Rethinking War and Peace

Rethinking
War and Peace

Diana Francis

Pluto Press

LONDON • ANN ARBOR, MI

First published 2004 by Pluto Press
345 Archway Road, London N6 5AA
and 839 Greene Street, Ann Arbor MI 48106, USA

www.plutobooks.com

British Library Cataloguing in Publication Data
A catalogue record for this book is available from the British Library

ISBN   0 7453 2188 7 hardback
ISBN   0 7453 2187 9 paperback

Library of Congress Cataloging in Publication Data applied for

10 9 8 7 6 5 4 3 2 1

Designed and produced for Pluto Press by
Chase Publishing Services, Fortescue, Sidmouth, EX10 9QG, England
Typeset from disk by Stanford DTP Services, Northampton, England
Printed and bound in the European Union by
Antony Rowe Ltd, Chippenham and Eastbourne, England

For my grandchildren

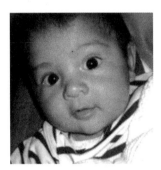

*and for all the people of my parents' generation
who never gave up on their commitment to peace*

Contents

Acknowledgements

To Anne Rogers for her generous and unfailing help – editorial and technical – and for staying with me through the struggle of writing. I would not have survived without her.

To my parents, both long dead, for the values, beliefs and commitment, to which they were so faithful and which they handed on to me.

To my husband Nick, for his tolerance of my obsession with this book and for his moral support, general knowledge and good sense.

To Hugh Miall for his initial encouragement and cogent advice.

To Michael Randle and Brian Phillips, for their patient reading, helpful information and wise suggestions.

To Tony Kempster and Khalid Kishtainy for their advice on Just War theory, in Christianity and Islam respectively.

To Bruce Kent and the Movement for the Abolition of War, for being there and for furnishing me with many of the quotations I have used.

To Pluto Press for agreeing to publish this book and for being both accommodating and supportive.

To all those friends who have provided small but timely help when I have needed it.

Introduction

The plain fact is that the planet does not need more successful people. But it does desperately need more peacemakers, healers, restorers, storytellers, and lovers of every kind. It needs people who live well in their places. It needs people of moral courage willing to join the fight to make the world habitable and humane. And these qualities have little to do with success as our culture has defined it.

David Orr, *Earth in Mind*

I was born in 1944 to conscientious objector parents who had held on to their beliefs in spite of the terrible events of World War II and in the face of much social opprobrium. At the age of about 15, beginning with what I had learned from my parents, I began to develop my own understanding of pacifism, to some extent through reading but more through endless conversations and by listening to speeches and sermons. I became active in the antinuclear movement and in the local branch of The International Fellowship of Reconciliation (IFOR, of which I later became President) – an organisation which supports groups in different parts of the world that are resisting tyranny and militarism and working for justice through nonviolent action. The people I met in IFOR filled out my understanding of what it means to renounce violence without giving up on the struggle for humanity – indeed, as part of that struggle.

For the past dozen years I have worked as a trainer and facilitator in the field of 'conflict resolution', in many different parts of the world afflicted by the violence of war (work that is described in my first book, *People, Peace and Power*[1]). Although this work is important to me, and seems both urgent and necessary, the events of 11 September and all that has followed have taken me back to the point where I began: to the conviction that unless we address the *system* of war and the injustice it perpetuates, I and people like me are doomed to spend the rest of our days in frantic and ineffectual firefighting, in which one blaze is replaced by another, or is quelled only to break out again with renewed ferocity. At the same time the hidden violence of economic exploitation and

1

oppression, maintained by military might – whose effects are as dire as those of war – will not only continue but increase.

We are, as a species, at a crossroads: a point where we must choose. We have probably never felt less secure, more uncertain. We seem to be caught on a 'moving walkway' that has run out of control and is propelling us along so fast that we can hardly think, let alone find a way of stopping the conveyor belt while we collect our wits and see what is to be done. It is my belief that we need to get off it somehow, and fast, before it hurls us all 'together into the abyss'.[2]

The word 'pacifist' has an old-fashioned ring and is associated by most people with irrelevant idealism. Often, indeed, it is used as a derogatory term. While some regard pacifists as worthy souls, to be respected if not taken seriously, others see them as self-indulgent and dishonest, refusing to face the harsh realities of the world we inhabit. Because they resist war as a system, it is inferred that they are unconcerned with the real circumstances of particular wars.

Yet if we refuse to reconsider the fundamental assumptions that underlie the justification and acceptance of war, we shall remain caught in a dynamic of cruelty and destruction that will know no end, that undermines all that makes for human happiness, decency and meaning and that could lead to our destruction as a species.

Saying no to war, on the other hand, could be the first step in saying yes to a very different future. Why does it seem so impossible? Precisely because war is an integral part of a historic and pervasive system within which we are enmeshed, because we have always seen it as inevitable, and because recent events make it seem even more so.

Since 11 September 2001, while rejecting the cruel violence of such terrible assaults, I have joined with others in the struggle to resist the relentless rhetoric and momentum of the 'War on Terror'.[3] In so doing I have come to see more clearly than ever that to protest in an *ad hoc* way against individual wars is not enough. The military machine is far too powerful and integral to global economic domination to be stopped by anti-war movements that fade once a particular war is over and struggle to get under way again as the next calamity looms and peak too late to prevent it. And, as things stand, it seems there are too many vested interests and too much inertia within the current system for particular wars to be stopped – even when a majority opposes them. Our 'democracies' have proved themselves unresponsive to their people.

What is needed is a massive and sustained movement away from war *as such*, and towards constructive approaches to collective human relationships. This will entail a fundamental change in the way the world is organised and in prevailing approaches to power. This is indeed an ambitious project, but vital nonetheless. War must be seen for what it is: a human catastrophe, a violation of humanity. It 'must cease to be an admissible human institution'.[4]

It must cease to be an admissible human institution because people matter. They matter more than wealth or power or convenience, and they matter unconditionally. As human beings we owe each other, without question, respect for the dignity and needs that are inherent in our humanity.

Without this assumption no morality is possible, and morality is necessary to our wellbeing, as individuals and as a species. Since we exist in interdependence with all species and indeed all beings, we must learn to embrace them in our morality. It is our moral capacity, and our ability to care and suffer, to celebrate and create, that make us matter so much. Our ability to hurt and to harm is the other side of that capacity for good. The institution of war is an expression of our negative capacity and inflicts terrible harm on people and on the earth itself.

Writing this book has been a struggle. My mind has felt atomised by the sheer senselessness of what has been said and done. Much of my time and energy have been consumed by the need to take action to resist the madness of it all. And the difficulty I have experienced in finding the mental space to stop, think and write, while at the same time coping with and responding to the immediate crisis, is my own small version of a much wider dilemma. How can we manage the realities of now, while working towards a different set of realities for the future? How can we take out the military props when we don't seem to have a system that can stand up without them? How can we disentangle militarism from the terrible inequities it protects and promotes? These questions are at the heart of the challenge that I wish to address.

I believe we have the capacity to choose against war and so to give peace a chance: that to want to do so is a sign of sanity rather than madness; that the first step is to understand that there is a choice, and that we can and should make it. My purpose, then, is to undertake a radical re-examination of the assumption that war is either acceptable or inevitable, and to try to suggest some ways out of the apparently endless cycle of violence. This will involve reflections on human nature, society and ethics, on alternatives to war and on the values and nature of peace.

I am aware that my assumptions and perceptions will inevitably (despite all my travels and cross-cultural friendships) be those of someone who has grown up in the West. The content of my arguments and the examples I give will be influenced by my own context and experience, and by my preoccupation with what I see as the damaging and fundamentally immoral behaviour of the world's most powerful nations. Indeed, I believe that we should all, wherever we live, focus first and foremost on what is done in our own society and in our name. But I also know that I am part of a growing counter-culture – one that has global dimensions – and that in much of what I say I will be voicing the opinions of a great many people in very different parts of the world. This book is for them too.

As the book's title suggests, I am attempting a fundamental review of the relationship between war and peace. Nonetheless, it is a response to the moment in which we live and the events of the past two or three years will receive a great deal of attention. It is those events that have brought me to the point of undertaking a task that I would not otherwise have imposed on myself. And it is those events that are likely to have prompted you to pick up this book. I see them as the apotheosis of militarism as a system and not an aberration.

Events are moving fast and by the time this is published it will already be out of date – by the time you read it even more so. It will remain a book of and for our time, but with (I hope) something fundamental to say about human relationships and the future of our planet.

Having spent my life being asked hard questions and trying to find answers to them, I am in no danger of assuming that to mount and sustain a fundamental challenge to war is an easy undertaking. In spite of the depth of my convictions, I have often doubted my ability to write cogently enough to be in any way convincing. I have feared that, however persuasive they are with me, my arguments would not hold up under the scrutiny of others. Worst of all, I have been afraid that I might myself come to find them unconvincing!

Recently, however, I read Jonathan Glover's brilliant book, *Humanity*:[5] a compassionate and cogent exploration of human cruelty and destructiveness on the one hand, and moral resources on the other. While in more than four hundred pages there is no discussion of the ethical justification for war as such, the whole book points to that question. Having been afraid that my reasoning would prove too weak to stand up in the light of such a work, I found that in the event it was reinforced by it.

In taking a position so far removed from accepted thinking on this subject, I shall be expected to provide answers to riddles never posed to those who justify war. Nonetheless, I choose to make the attempt. The way the last millennium ended and this one began has made such an endeavour feel like a human obligation. The title I have chosen is sweeping, reflecting the scale of the task. My hope is more modest: to contribute something, at least, to the wide and profound debate that needs to begin, urgently.

I shall not be arguing that anything can remove the fact of human frailty, with all its associated dilemmas. I *shall* be maintaining that to uphold certain fundamental values, through personal and collective policy and structures, is of paramount importance for our wellbeing and our survival, and that war cannot be part of that. And I shall be echoing Glover's hope that, given the belief and commitment of 'ordinary people', 'the ending of the festival of cruelty may be possible'.[6] War threatens our planet and all its inhabitants; peace will need to embrace them all and it is our responsibility.

1
Where Are We?

The time is out of joint.
William Shakespeare, *Hamlet*

EVENTS AND REALITIES

I write at a time of great turbulence and distress. It could be argued that no time has ever been otherwise, yet the first years of the third millennium do seem to have witnessed an extraordinary coming together of crises and exceptional displays of human ineptitude and brutality. In the last 15 years the cruel proxy wars and global tensions of the Cold War have been replaced by wars of secession, states on the verge of collapse, terrible regional wars for power and economic gain and control and inter-ethnic and sectarian violence of terrible ferocity.

At the same time we have been confronted with the full reality of the uncontested military and economic dominance of the US which has long had military bases in over 40 countries (including several in Britain) and now has them in every oil-producing and oil-distributing country in the world. The expression 'unipolar world' not only suggests the out-of-jointness of this state of affairs, but indicates a world view in which the reality of life beyond the shores of the US is scarcely recognised. This disregard is evidenced by the US refusal to be brought into the Kyoto climate change agreement or to recognise the jurisdiction of the International Criminal Court.

The events of 11 September 2001 came as a very great shock but perhaps, with hindsight, they should not have done. A world in which a wealthy elite in one nation (albeit in collusion with wealthy elites elsewhere) seeks to gain 'full spectrum dominance' – to control the entire planet and its resources (and even outer space) – is unlikely to be a safe or sustainable one. While the power of control may seem to be concentrated in a few hands, the desire for it is far more widely distributed and the resentment generated by attempted monopoly is infinite.

We are witnessing intensified polarisation between the West and 'the rest', one that is increasingly (however inaccurately) seen in terms of a confrontation between historic Christendom and the world of Islam. The notion and language of identity, particularly 'ethnic', 'cultural' and 'religious', now dominate discussion about conflict and justice. (I have put these terms in quotation marks because the concepts they represent are all – in my view rightly – contested.)

There were over 100 million war-related deaths in the twentieth century. In its last year, 110,000 people died in armed conflict.[1] Despite all legal conventions, civilians are the main casualties in modern warfare. In a world in which the possibility of man-made catastrophe seems ever more imminent, those who live in the rich world are increasingly 'risk averse' and the major military powers resort more and more to the kind of war-fighting that minimises losses among their own forces. It is as if war and death should no longer be associated. To this end the human 'enemy' is made more and more invisible in that knowledge of the numbers of their casualties is withheld.

At the same time, those who fight against overwhelming military odds are becoming ever more willing to face certain death in their bid to inflict damage. Once more civilians are the main casualties, and, even more importantly, the notion of military security loses its meaning. It is clear that a war is no answer to 'terror'. Moreover, the idea that war *is* terror is gaining ground.

I believe that the phenomenon of 'suicide bombing' brings into relief another fundamental reality: that material concerns do not hold the dominant position in the motivational hierarchy that modernists would argue. It would appear that feelings of affronted dignity and values can generate greater hatred than simple want or insecurity and that beliefs play a powerful role in motivating action. This is relevant not only to the consideration of war but also to any project for its abolition.

In the last two years, we have seen the supreme irony of countries that have spent the last five decades and more developing and accumulating ever more devastating weapons of mass destruction using any attempt by others to develop such weapons as a justification for unbridled military aggression. The only state on earth to have used nuclear weapons – one that has bombed 27 countries (some of them more than once) since World War II,[2] and covertly attacked many more – has seen fit to designate a collection of weak countries as a threat to the world's security.

Nuclear weapons certainly pose a threat. The proliferation predicted by the anti-nuclear movement from its very inception has indeed taken place and consequently the world is a more dangerous place. The collapse of the former Soviet Union has – as was also foreseen – made the acquisition of nuclear materials and technology more susceptible than ever to clandestine use. Despite the fact that there is now no plausible threat to the US, and in spite of the obligations of all nuclear weapons states under the nuclear non-proliferation treaty to work towards total nuclear disarmament, the arms race – with its virtually lone contender – continues unabated, with new attention being given to the development of 'useable' weapons on the one hand and space-based defence on the other. Britain, ever the compliant friend, is set to host vital elements of the 'Star Wars' system. Nuclear disarmament remains as urgent a need as ever and is an entirely possible project. It seems hard, nowadays, to imagine anyone outside the circles of power mania opposing it.

While the global peace which the UN was founded to promote seems further away than ever, the justice that would characterise it is no nearer. Indeed, the gap between rich and poor continues to grow. It is morally obscene that while poverty, famine, contaminated water, lack of basic health care and lack of education continue to blight the lives of millions, global military expenditure for 2002 amounted to $794 billion – *without the costs of war*.[3] Even the relatively paltry £2 billion that were agreed for tackling the scourge of AIDS in Africa have not been forthcoming. In wealthy Britain we 'cannot afford' to sustain a national health service or transport system or provide free tertiary education, and the care of the elderly – among other things – is starved of funds, yet £3 billion were set aside by the chancellor for the Iraq war (an amount that seems likely to have been exceeded).

The UN itself, whatever the vision of its founders, and notwithstanding some excellent work, remains the creation and tool of the globally powerful, and whatever credibility it has retained or won has been shredded, if not destroyed, by the scorn with which it has been treated by the US and its allies. The notion of a 'defensive pre-emptive strike', and the context in which it was used, have blown a gaping hole in international law.

Political violence and poverty have created a level of human migration that represents misery on a vast scale and has caused political friction and a degree of genuine social stress in the countries where those migrating – with whatever degree of compulsion or choice – arrive.

While children in unthinkable numbers are kidnapped and forced to fight, day-to-day violence against women and children continues on a shocking scale, amounting to a chronic, hidden war. Not only does it take place within the 'normal' structures of societies but illegal 'trafficking' has grown to epidemic proportions. While wars may divide most people, at the same time they open up routes and opportunities for this kind of exploitation.

The international arms trade, with a $21 billion turnover (excluding unauthorised trading, which is vast), continues to make the world more dangerous for its citizens, fuels wars and diverts much needed resources. To say that it provides jobs is no kind of moral justification and indeed the arms industry creates remarkably few jobs per pound. In the UK it is subsidised out of public funds, receiving 50 per cent of all export credit guarantees for what constitutes 2 per cent of all the country's exports.[4]

While states are still the primary wielders of military power, 'informal' armed violence is on the rise everywhere and civil wars are rife. Armed interventions by the US and others also challenge the notion of the integrity of states, and global businesses are usurping their power in many spheres. The 'military industrial complex'[5] remains alive and well, corrupting politics in every part of the world.

The US has secured control of Iraq's oil and will establish military bases there, so replacing those that are no longer viable in Saudi Arabia. But the political chaos and human misery in the Middle East go from bad to worse. The 'road map' has led nowhere and Arab bitterness has intensified. It is hard to see where all this will lead.

In other parts of the world – Chechnya, for instance, and Mindanao in the Philippines – the War on Terror has created a climate in which governments have felt free to deal with armed dissidents with greater than ever harshness, knowing that the US would give them tacit support. (In Sri Lanka, on the other hand, the proscription of the Tamil Tigers seems to have contributed to a ceasefire in the decades-old civil war.) In countries around the world, civil liberties have been under attack and human rights violated in the name of security.

Technology has done much to improve human life, but our technological aptitude is not matched by our wisdom or sense of responsibility for consequences. A culture of personal gratification and instant satisfaction has seen a relentless rise not only in military threat but in ecological exploitation and destruction, in waste and pollution. While the health of all of us is threatened, the earth is being littered and contaminated and the climate is changing inexorably. As with any threat, it is the poor who have the least protection and who are suffering most.

Not only is our technological genius accompanied by folly – and cruelty – it is also paralleled by carelessness and ineptitude. During the war on Iraq, most of the 'coalition' troops who died were killed by 'friendly fire'. 'Smart bombs' strayed into neighbouring countries, landing in Syria, Turkey and Iran. And now the whirlwind that is being reaped in Iraq has placed coalition soldiers in situations they simply cannot handle, despite all their weaponry.

Since the bombing of the 'Twin Towers' and the Pentagon and the launching of the War on Terror, the terrible grip of violence on our global society has been brought into the forefront of our attention – even for those of us whose daily lives have seemed very safe. While the war on Afghanistan brought many thousands more deaths to its people, for most Afghans it brought neither peace nor development. Since the recent war on Iraq (which most Afghans, having tasted the ashes of 'liberation', fiercely opposed) devastated that already ruined country, removing its dictator but bringing chaos, the elusive forces of terror – and their support – have been augmented and new attacks have taken place. The UK Parliamentary Select Committee on 'defence' has concluded that the war on Iraq got in the way of addressing the threat from Al Qaeda and made Britain less rather than more secure. The political price is beginning to be paid both here and in the US.

While the war on Afghanistan was widely opposed outside the West, the war on Iraq was fought against the wishes of a vast and vocal majority of Europeans, who made common cause with the millions who opposed it around the world (including the US) and held demonstrations of unprecedented size in a vast and sustained campaign. This opposition has not only been sustained but has increased since the war, especially in the US. This movement is significant not only because of its magnitude and concertedness, but also because it took shape in a context of deepening cynicism about politics and politicians – across the world, including not only established 'democratic' countries but those emerging from decades of Soviet control and those that have never known anything other than colonialism, corruption and tyranny. While the anti-war movement expressed this disaffection, it also was a sign that the worm can turn – disaffected and apparently supine populations can spring into life and take to the streets.

The level of public engagement was, I believe, unprecedented and here in the UK for once the media took notice. Though for a long time it was apparently unnoticed by the BBC, this time the scale of the movement was such that it eventually could not be ignored and, as the war on Iraq approached, radio, TV and newspapers kept the issue and related events constantly in the forefront. (It would be interesting to know if anyone has monitored public health and the frequency of stress-related illnesses in the West since 11 September.) The peace movement failed to prevent the war on Iraq – maybe earlier coverage would have made a difference. But its analysis and predictions have been so plainly vindicated that it is possible that there may at last be some delayed recognition that it has been right in the past, too, and that it should be taken seriously now.

PRESENTATION AND PERCEPTIONS

In my school days, history presented war as a vista of grand sweeps and movements in which heroic battles were won and lost, political geography made and remade, nations constructed and deconstructed. In the war paintings of past ages, though the carnage of battle may be portrayed, the paintings are heroic in style as well as scale. The human experience of war is not their focus. And in the centres of (Western) cities, men on horseback brandish swords triumphantly, honoured, it seems, for their naked, violent power, rather than their humanity.

War memorials of the last century are more sombre, recording deaths or depicting weary soldiers weighed down with heavy packs and guns. The poets of World Wars I and II drew their readers into the hellish realities they endured and the huge questions which these engendered. Nowadays it would seem unthinkable to depict war directly in triumphal statuary. The acts of human violence of which war consists have become an embarrassment. There is, as recent events have shown, a growing sense of unease about war as an instrument of human aspirations – a growing awareness of the moral norms it breaches. And yet military leadership still holds its place as the archetype of heroism and greatness.

It is one of the great ironies of the twentieth century that the unprecedented scale and destructiveness of war was accompanied by ever-growing revulsion or moral squeamishness in the face of its effects. That could, of course, be put the other way round: that in spite of growing moral concerns, war not only flourished as an institution but became ever more terrible in scale and brutality. Either way, the two trends ran in parallel. In the war on Iraq, some UK soldiers, it seems, had not been prepared for the realities of what they would be asked to do and refused orders. A military commentator remarked that maybe in recent years we had put too much emphasis on the professional training that military service could offer and not made recruits sufficiently aware of the fact that one day they could be under orders to kill.

In the past, geographical remoteness helped to distance people from the hideous effects of war. Distance still attenuates their reality. The glorious tranquillity of the spring days in England during the early stages of the Iraq war made its horror seem far away and unreal – even to those of us who so passionately opposed it, watched every news bulletin and were constantly and oppressively aware of what was happening. Though unspeakable violence was being committed in our name, our own lives continued in safety and prosperity, and this both intensified and assuaged the pain.

Wars in which the West plays no visible part still receive scant attention here and impinge very little on popular consciousness. Nonetheless, the growth in public communications in the past century has shrunk the globe and led to an inevitable growth in public awareness of war and its realities. It has made *people* more aware of each other, so that those who rule them cannot so easily hide the effects of their actions.

To minimise the impact of knowledge and the scale of potential public revolt against the wars they wish to justify, Western politicians have invented a euphemistic vocabulary for their presentation. In this great enterprise of deception, emotion is dressed up as reason and reason as emotion. So the expression 'fired in anger', as applied to weapons of war, means to fire them 'for real', rather than in a practice exercise. But the anger alluded to is not real, or certainly, in the 'proper' conduct of war, not decisive. One US rocket launcher vehicle used in Iraq was named 'Anger Management'. Terms suggesting righteous human emotion are used as an implied justification for actions taken, which by the same token are framed as measured and responsible.

The murderous acts of 11 September were met with genuine grief, anger and outrage and demanded a rational response. But thereafter those feelings were used as a cover for manipulation and duplicity. In the run-up to the recent war on Iraq (and before that on Afghanistan), there was much feigning of emotion, particularly on the part of President Bush and his close colleagues, while Tony Blair's chosen emotional style was one more of earnest concern and passionate determination than of anger.

These studied emotions were used to cover the increasingly contradictory and implausible nature of the 'reasons' given for launching a war against an already ruined country. Ironically, one powerful and original cause of the war on Afghanistan was probably an emotional one: the need to hit back at someone after 11 September and to be seen to be powerful rather than vulnerable. But a cloak of reason was stitched together (with many alterations) to provide these impulses with decent clothing. When those reasons in turn proved unconvincing, fake emotion was added to make them more impressive.

Acts of deadly violence in war – bombardment, wholesale destruction, mutilation, incineration, reduction to rubble, mass killing, massacre, devastation, laying waste – are referred to as 'conflict', 'force', 'intervention'. Starting a war is described as 'becoming operational' and, in a step still further from reality, the verb 'to war-game' has been invented ('the enemy is different from the one we'd war-gamed'.[6] The term 'collateral damage', now infamous, epitomises a linguistic approach which creates distance and distracts us with technical language, disguising the random, huge impact of massive weaponry with words such as 'clinical', 'surgical' and 'precision'. (Is the 'theatre' of war a surgical or dramatic theatre?) The most massive and devastating bombs – short of nuclear bombs – are called 'daisy cutters'. The expression 'shock and awe', which might well have been called a 'blitzkrieg', seemed designed to invest the proposed onslaught with the god-like qualities of power and being above morality.

Sometimes the language of war reveals rather than disguises its true nature, being not only impersonal (and therefore inhumane) but brutal. The US talk of 'decapitating the regime' of Saddam Hussein, while referring to an institution, nonetheless employed a chilling human image which is all too close to reality. When we were told that Iraq's Republican Guard were to be 'softened up', the metaphor was at the same time euphemistic, ghoulish and boastful. Carrying out raids into Baghdad before it was 'taken' was 'a poke in the eye' for the Iraqi regime. (The word 'regime' is reserved for enemy governments.)

These linguistic games are symptomatic of modern ambivalence about war: the wish to justify it – even boast about it – and rouse support for it, and at the same time an awareness of its ugliness and of the way it contravenes all the civil norms with which Western nations like to associate themselves. The modern version of the old war myth needs to cater for modern sensitivities. It was striking to contrast the rhetoric of the 'Coalition' with the blood-curdling pronouncements of the Ba'ath Party leadership as it faced eradication. These contained only the crudeness of bellicosity, undisguised by techno-speak or the understated arrogance of overwhelming violent power.

Perhaps the most fundamental linguistic device for sanitising war is to dehumanise the people fighting 'on the other side' by describing them simply as 'the enemy' – in contrast to 'our boys' (the few women soldiers largely hidden in this) and as husbands, fathers and brothers. 'Our own' fighters have human faces and identities, but those of 'the enemy' do not. Our own dead are counted and grieved over; the enemy dead are not. They cease to exist. Occasionally their number is publicised as a matter for rejoicing. More often than not it is not mentioned – apparently being of no concern. The two to three hundred thousand Iraqi soldiers killed in the spring of 2003 – usually dismissed as 'irregular militia', 'terrorists' or 'criminals' – were scarcely ever mentioned. (I find that hard to grasp – unbearably poignant: that so many should die so quickly in such a relentless and overwhelming attack, their bodies broken in no less terrible a way than those of civilians, and that no one should even mention them. But of course their families have felt the full impact of their loss. It has not passed unnoticed.)

'Us–them' language not only disguises the brutality and human significance of what is done but constitutes the most elementary expression of a moral justification for what in any other terms is unacceptable. In killing 'the enemy' we are doing good, not committing homicide. On the Coalition side, military entry into a country and the massive bombardment of its towns and cities were presented not as an invasion but as an act of liberation. Those who resisted it were not defenders but oppressors. I remember a British journalist reporting with some shock that the Coalition forces were being referred to in Arabic news media as 'the invaders' and Iraqi soldiers as 'defenders'.

Not only are the language and presentation of war used to disguise its true nature, but the content of what is communicated is (necessarily) highly selective. For instance, those who watched Al Jazeera TV news saw a very different coverage from that seen on terrestrial UK channels, for instance, or on CNN. They were shown far more images of death and destruction, as against moments of apparent triumph of the 'good guys'. (The construction of this picture may itself involve great selectivity and indeed deliberate falsification – like the wrecking of the statue of Saddam Hussein in Baghdad, which was staged for reporters by a small group of 'extras' and the shots and photographs doctored to give the appearance of a large crowd.)

Once a war has been started, its logic and dynamics are hard to escape. From then on, it is more comfortable to try and think positively about what is being done. To oppose it is to be considered treacherous. Here again, however, there seems to have been some shift, in that concern over civilian casualties, at least, is seen as legitimate. (When the acclaimed German writer, Gunther Grass,[7] was interviewed about his new novel describing the suffering of German civilians during World War II, he said that until now this had not been deemed an acceptable focus for exploration, or even record.)

Concern was assiduously expressed by those speaking for the US and UK military and governments for the preservation of civilian safety in Iraq (in no small measure in response to worldwide anti-war feeling). We were told that everything had been done to avoid civilian targets, but that 'shock and awe' were not discriminate. When it came to military choices, the commitment to avoid civilian deaths was outweighed by the desire to protect 'our own' soldiers. Hence the justification of the use of cluster bombs, for instance, or the massive bombardments that preceded the entry of Coalition forces into Baghdad; and hence the fact that the relatively few deaths of Coalition soldiers received far greater attention than the many deaths of civilian Iraqis.

In this recent Iraq war, the term 'propaganda warfare' was aptly used. When language fails to disguise reality and where that reality is particularly unacceptable or disadvantageous, more direct forms of deception are used. Early in 2003, according to an aid worker I met who had recently come from Afghanistan, the bodies of US soldiers killed in the fighting with warlords were stored rather than sent home, in order to minimise public awareness of the ongoing losses to US troops. With preparations for another war under way, it was important to disguise the realities of the continued fighting and chaos in much of that devastated country after the supposed establishment of peace and democracy.

Deceptions may be revealed once a war is over – sometimes sooner, as when it was falsely claimed that Saddam Hussein rather than the US had bombed the market in Baghdad. But in the midst of war there is a public tendency to believe the best, because the worst is so miserably uncomfortable. At the time of the sinking of the Argentinian ship the *Belgrano* in the Falklands war it was denied that the ship had been attacked while in retreat, though the fact was later admitted. Yet this did not seem to make the UK public less gullible when new lies were told, for instance about the bombing of bridges and trains in the later war on Serbia.[8]

In such instances truths emerge eventually but their effect is neutralised by time. At other times the public is duped by retrospective lies. For instance, the mass exodus of Albanian Kosovars from Kosovo took place after the bombing of Serbia began, but was (within days) presented as if it had been the trigger *for* the bombing. In another breathtaking reinvention of events in their immediate aftermath, Tony Blair asserted that it was the French opposition to a new Security Council resolution designed to trigger a war on Iraq that prevented a diplomatic solution that would have made war unnecessary. In reality all the British Prime Minister's diplomatic efforts were devoted to gathering support for a war, not for its avoidance.

Unless listeners and viewers are alert and critical, lies loudly proclaimed and often repeated are remarkably easily received as truth, despite contradictory evidence from the immediate or more distant past, or in the small print of today's news. Once the most intense fighting and dramatic events are over, the news peters out. Most of us do not realise that Kosovo has not become the multi-ethnic democracy that was promised and still has no viable status, or that fighting and lawlessness continue in Afghanistan. It is only because of the scale of resistance to the war on Iraq and the consequent newsworthiness and political impact of the truths that are seeping out that awareness of the terrible situation there is relatively wide.

It is to be hoped that this will prove a turning point in public awareness of war and concern at its consequences. Despite all the lies and subterfuges and 'economies' with the truth, some at least of the terrible realities of war are being brought into our living rooms. Once the demand for this kind of coverage is clear, the media will, I believe, increasingly provide it. Moreover, the stories that were not meant to be told now reach us by email from all around the globe, and new sources of information are available to us on the internet. The control of information has passed out of the hands of governments and media barons. The genie is out of the bottle. At this point the moral argument becomes more acute than ever. The battle for hearts and minds has become a war.

2
What is War Good For?
Myth and Reality

I am tired and sick of war. Its glory is all moonshine. War is hell.

General Sherman, 1879

More frequently than not it leads to fresh wars. Preparing for war never seems to prevent it, but rather to precipitate it; and in its conclusions war is just about as disastrous to the victor as to the vanquished.

Field Marshal Sir William Robertson, 1929

A war is not like an earthquake or a tornado. It is an act of men and women ... Do not let people lead you to think for a moment that war is a necessary institution.

Jessie Wallace Hughan

Peace has been a dream from generation to generation. It is my dream. Why does it prove so illusive? I believe that war is more than a sign that so far we have failed to achieve our dream but that it is integral to a system that makes peace impossible. If peace is ever to become a reality, it is a prime necessity to deconstruct the myth of war's necessity, legitimacy and power for good.

THE MYTH OF WAR

In the run-up to the recent war on Iraq, we were subjected, for months, to the daily question, 'Is war inevitable?' – as if this war were an asteroid inexorably heading towards us, rather than a deliberate and resolute plan to act in a certain way. Nonetheless, many people believe that war is sometimes *morally* inevitable. This conviction is based on what I would argue to be a myth: that war is what works, the 'means of last resort' – the one thing that we can rely on when all else fails. This myth is based on three false assumptions. The first is that leaders are trying to do things that really need to be done: that the causes for which they go to war are just. The second is that they do really try everything else before going to war – that all alternatives are exhausted. The third is that war is effective in achieving the good goals claimed as their causes.

This threefold war myth is so firmly established that it is hardly ever questioned at a fundamental level. The propaganda machines work overtime to perpetuate it, and because it is a complex myth it is hard to deconstruct. However, it must be taken apart and shown to be hollow – and poisonous – if we are ever to escape from its hold on us and from the grip of war as a system. We shall never be able to pursue peace in any consistent way until that is done. That is what I want to do in this chapter.

There is such widespread cynicism about the rationale for the War on Terror and the effects of the wars on Afghanistan and Iraq that I shall not dwell on them at length. But since they are so present and so relevant I will begin with them, before going on to a wider discussion of the myth's three distinct elements.

In the cases of both Afghanistan and Iraq, security was the given reason for war. In the former case, however, little time was wasted on reasoning, and the impression was given that the initial motive was to hit back at someone after the devastating attacks on the 'Twin Towers' and the Pentagon. Assuming Al Qaeda was indeed the group responsible for the attacks (and this no longer seems to be disputed) and that the goal was to eliminate them, the idea would have been rather ill-conceived since they are not the kind of local and limited organisation that could be wiped out in a localised counter-attack. Those responsible for the atrocities of 11 September did not come from Afghanistan, nor did they prepare their 'mission' from there. If they had, a general war against the Taliban regime was not the best way of eliminating them and in the event did not succeed even locally.

Once the war on Afghanistan had been launched, however, a new reason was brought in to justify it: the removal of a cruel and despotic regime. What was not mentioned was that the same regime had been supported in the past as a counter to Russian hegemony. Nor was it acknowledged that the warlords drawn in to fight for the US had been equally disastrous when in power. Extending its economic and political control in a region key to the future of oil supplies seems the only convincing long-term goal for this choice of action by the US. (I will not get embroiled here with conspiracy theories, though they are not without cogency and have been expounded by remarkably sane people.)[1]

Before the war on Afghanistan was launched it was suggested that negotiations with the Taliban regime could have resulted in their no longer allowing Al Qaeda's activities within the country. It became clear, however, that the US had no interest in 'exhausting all alternatives' to war – quite the contrary, for the reasons given above.

The war's outcome, in terms of its initially proclaimed goal of security, has been negative. Osama bin Laden remains an icon of *jihad* against Western imperialism. There is no evidence that Al Qaeda has been weakened, and terrorist attacks continue around the world. Terrorism cannot be bombed out of existence. It is a part of the dynamic of violence and disrespect that requires little in terms of personnel and weaponry. It can spring up anywhere at any time.

In terms of the post-hoc reason brought in to justify the war – the 'liberation' of Afghanistan – the picture remains bleak. At the end of October 2003 it was being reported that the country was experiencing the worst fighting since the overthrow of the Taliban.[2] Human rights – particularly in the case of women – continue to be violated and warlords continue to hold sway. This is hardly surprising. The model of human relations that the US has enacted is not one of democratic process and respect for human rights but one of bullying and violence – the very things it claimed to be addressing.

The war on Iraq, like the war on Afghanistan, was initially justified in the name of security. When that argument proved unconvincing (and we have seen how little justification there was for the claims of an imminent threat from weapons of mass destruction [WMD]) the 'regime change' cause was deployed. We were told that the war was being fought in order to liberate Iraq's people from a cruel tyrant. As with Afghanistan, no mention was made of past connivance, support and military assistance. Furthermore, as with Afghanistan, oil and other strategic interests seem the only plausible explanation – along with 'national pride'.

Far from valiant attempts to exhaust all alternatives to war, what we saw was a ruthless determination to brush such attempts aside and the relentless pursuit of the war option in the face of overwhelming world opinion against it. When the war was declared to be over, George Bush told his troops, 'Through you the dignity of a great nation has been restored'[3] – revealing that this war, like the one on Afghanistan, was an opportunity to re-assert 'full spectrum dominance'. Unsurprisingly, the great majority of Afghans opposed the war on Iraq.

Though one US spokesperson said it was 'very difficult to fault the war',[4] once again war's result in security terms has not been as advertised. No WMD have been found. The country remains extremely unstable and has become an international forum for attacking the US, while its own citizens bear the brunt of the suffering – orphans eke out an existence, girls dare not go to school for fear of kidnap and rape, shootings and explosions are commonplace. Even humanitarian agencies are under attack. As I write (in late November 2003), the UN has pulled out the last of its foreign nationals and far more US servicemen have been killed since the war 'ended' than while it was officially under way. Terrorist attacks against British interests in Turkey have been related to the war on Iraq and to Turkey's perceived collusion with the US and the UK.

On the other hand the US has the opportunity of establishing several new military bases, so compensating for less certain military relations with Saudi Arabia and furthering its strategic aim of regional hegemony. US companies are now in charge of the oil, Iraq is generally 'open for business' and US 'defence' companies with close ties to the US administration have announced substantial increases in profitability.

In both Afghanistan and Iraq we have seen a military strategy deliberately chosen by the US and used to extend its control: a strategy that is so risky that it may backfire and one that has little to do with countering terrorism or with what most people would call peace. In both wars the arms industry has prospered and through both wars lucrative contracts have been won by vast US-based companies who have been assigned the many tasks of reconstruction created by years of war, neglect, sanctions (in Iraq's case) and more war.

I would now like to focus on the first of the three false assumptions that make up the war myth, looking more broadly at different types of war and the reasons for which they are waged. I will start with a general discussion about war and its cause, and then look specifically at the motivations of war leaders.

WAR'S CAUSES

The word 'cause' in this context has at least two meanings. We can ask, 'What was the cause of this war?', meaning what circumstances, events, decisions or actions occasioned it. Or we can ask, 'For what cause was this war fought?', meaning what were the purposes of those who waged it. It is hard to keep these two meanings distinct, since causes of the latter kind are often related to causes in the former sense. Furthermore, as I will argue, the goals war leaders claim for a war may not be the real ones, or at most partly so. And they themselves may stumble rather than march into war.

Wars – 'hostile contention by means of armed forces'[5] – are fought between states and within states; for a wide variety of 'causes' in both senses of the word; on different scales, geographically and numerically; at different intensities and over different lengths of time; with different degrees of popular support, and with different kinds of weapons. One thing they have in common, however: they are all destructive. For this reason they should not be confused with conflict, which may be 'waged' constructively and without violence. All too often, though, war is the form that conflict takes.

Wars may be categorised in a variety of ways. One attractively simple typology makes a fundamental distinction between 'interstate' and 'non-interstate' wars. It subdivides the latter into three categories. One embraces those fought for revolution/ ideology, to change states – for instance from capitalist to communist (or vice versa), from secular to religious (or vice versa), or from dictatorship to democracy. Another comprises those fought on the grounds of identity, including struggles for access to wealth, employment and social and political participation, and for autonomy, control or secession. The third category is labelled as 'factional', including *'coups d'état*, intra-elite power struggles, brigandage, criminality and warlordism, where the aim is to usurp, seize or retain state power merely to further particular interests'.[6]

This typology provides us with a useful starting point and helps us to distinguish between different types of intrastate war. But like any other typology, of necessity it suggests clearer distinctions between types of war than in fact exist, masking the overlaps between them. For instance, it does not represent the phenomenon of 'proxy wars' in which the interests of outsiders are played out in civil wars, and the different motivations for intrastate war are often mixed. I shall begin this general review of causes by looking at the motives of outsiders in 'intrastate' wars, go on to discuss their internal motivations, and conclude with a brief look at interstate wars as such and a post-script on terrorism.

Our focus here is on the causes of wars and the purposes claimed for them – whether they can be described as just or moral. Factional wars seem to be ruled out by definition, since they are fought 'lawlessly', for reasons of greed and self-interest. I believe the term 'factional', or at least its moral content, could be applied equally to most wars fought by states, as well as within them.

As many writers have observed, wars within states have predominated over recent decades. Since the end of the Soviet Empire, civil wars in former Communist countries have proliferated. But during the Cold War the two big powers were indeed at war by proxy in 'internal conflicts' in different parts of the world in which they were covertly involved, pursuing their policies and interest through them. Now the US and its allies have embarked on a new series of overt wars in other states in order to change them in line with their own policies. These are called 'wars of intervention'.

A high proportion of recent wars fought within states have been fomented by interested individuals in weak, corrupt, factionalised or 'failing' states. Often the imposition of 'economic restructuring' by the International Monetary Fund (IMF) and the consequent impoverishment of a country's people and services contribute to such failure and instability, not to mention the human misery behind it. (For instance, IMF policy in Sierra Leone contributed to its becoming a net importer of rice rather than a net exporter.) The big powers have alternately ignored, promoted (more or less covertly), or condemned civil wars, depending where their vested interests lay. If the status quo is generally favourable to the West, 'moderation' and 'conflict resolution' may be encouraged.

In different countries, the US in particular has stimulated and supported insurgency against left-wing governments and given military assistance to right-wing 'counter-insurgency measures', for instance in Angola, Afghanistan and Iran, the Philippines and Indonesia, and most of Latin America. Ghana's President Nkrumah was overthrown because of economic interests and Congo was destabilised by the West for economic and political reasons.

Although such activities were at their height during the Cold War, they have not gone away. One current example of this policy is the US programme in Colombia. US involvement in the suppression of guerrilla activity in Mindanao, the Philippines, is another – quite apart from the invasion of Afghanistan and Iraq. All these interventions have been 'hegemonic'. In many countries the use of private armies by multinational corporations makes them major military as well as economic players.

Arms exports from the West into regions ravaged by armed conflict have been extremely high. The war in the Congo where, at the time of writing, more than 4 million have been killed (most of them civilians) has been fuelled by a steady flow of arms from outside. This in itself is a cynical and lucrative form of intervention. The cost of the arms trade to the world's poorest has been indescribable, in terms of diverted resources, the disruption of productive activity and in direct casualties – again, mostly civilian.

Wars of secession within the former Soviet Union have proliferated since the collapse of Communism. Since these disturb the status quo – 'business as usual' – and offer no advantages to the West, the aspirations to independence of those who fight them are not a matter of concern. While the US has supported (and indeed fomented) bloody revolutions in many countries in order to remove regimes inimical to its own interests, the West favours the preservation of existing state boundaries. Its concern is with the stability needed for the promotion of its own economic interests and political influence.

Western intervention in the former Yugoslavia, when it came, was a response prompted not only by public unease about a war fought in back gardens not dissimilar to our own but also by the West's strategic interests in the political and geographical interface between what used to be called Western Europe and the Arab world. (How widely is it known that Kosovo is now home to a huge US base with a 99-year lease?) It was in sharp contrast to the West's minimal response to the terrible civil wars that have torn post-colonial Africa apart. At the level of governments, these seem to have excited shockingly little concern. Presumably cost-benefit analysis showed intervention to hold no advantages and there was no appreciable political pressure for action to be taken.

Sometimes neighbouring states have pursued their own interests in civil wars, too – as in the Congo, where, since the death of President Mobutu, neighbouring countries have become embroiled, whether in pursuit of armed groups posing a threat to their own security or with an eye to the country's vast mineral wealth.

There has been much recent debate, within the world of 'conflict studies', as to the relative importance of 'greed' and 'grievance' as motives for war.[7] Civil wars or 'insurgency' may take place for a variety of reasons, which could be plotted somewhere along an imaginary line between greed and grievance. Very often (if not always) there is a ground of exclusion or oppression in which the seeds of war are sown. For those who are on the receiving end of aggression and repression, security, liberty and just access to the things necessary for their wellbeing are evidently an urgent need and recourse may be taken to guerrilla tactics, sometimes amounting to civil war. In other situations, disaffection manifests itself in sporadic terrorism, sometimes over many years.

Resources are a classic war interest: the need (or desire) to acquire land, diamonds, oil or water. As populations increase and living standards rise, scarcities look set to increase, and with them, arguably, the likelihood of conflict. However, archaeological findings suggest that scarcity is a matter of unequal distribution of resources within societies – as one anthropologist (Brian Ferguson) put it, 'a matter of politics and economics, rather than the twin bugbears of too many people and not enough to go round'.[8] The sad irony is that the discovery of exportable resources in a 'poor' country makes it likely not that it will prosper but rather that it will become subject to violent conflict and that its people will be further impoverished.[9]

Neocolonial wars, aimed at political and economic control, can be seen as greedy wars. And the 'military industrial complex', which stands to gain directly from war itself (rather than from its outcome) is driven by greed. It cannot therefore be assumed that the pre-eminent purpose of those engaged in war is always to win it. Sometimes they have an interest in perpetuating it. In Sierra Leone and Uganda, for instance, many of those involved in the fighting have gained financially, whether from the spoils of war or from trading controlled by it, and have colluded in contriving the war's continuation in order to go on doing so.[10]

However, resources and just access to them also constitute a legitimate concern for governments and different sectors of their populations. Along with human rights violations perpetrated by oppressive governments and those they employ to control their people, poverty is in many countries a genuine and profound grievance. Those who seek to understand and articulate the dynamics of oppression do so through ideological frameworks and fight 'wars of liberation' under political banners. Though inter-group dynamics and personal ambitions may cloud the purity of their motives and the methods used by such movements may be no better than those used in other wars, issues of justice may be seen as underlying them.

Though civil wars are often seen and described as 'identity wars', ethnic, cultural and religious differences are not in themselves a 'cause' of war – as vividly illustrated by this commentary on the recent re-emergence of violent conflict in Burundi:

> If Burundi's war was ever motivated primarily by ethnic hatred, that day is long past. It started in 1993, after the country's first Hutu president was assassinated by renegade Tutsi soldiers. Tribal massacres followed, but the conflict has since then morphed into a struggle for power, and so for control over Burundi's ridiculously meagre resources. Some of the worst acts of brutality have been committed by Hutus against other Hutus: the mainly Hutu rebels are now fighting a government that is headed by a Hutu.[11]

Sometimes 'identity' is used as a rallying point for ambitious politicians; sometimes it does indeed contribute to misunderstanding, clashing values and alienation; sometimes discrimination, exclusion and violence meted out on the grounds of identity can constitute the grievance that provides the tinder for smouldering violence or a conflagration.

In situations of abrupt and radical change, with a consequent loss of any previous inclusive identity and political and economic instability, this in turn may provide the opportunity for demagogues like Slobodan Milosevic or Franjo Tudjman to spark a war for their own purposes of aggrandisement. The organisation and intensification of the 'ethnic' wars in Yugoslavia was justified in the name of liberation from oppression. Just how oppressive Yugoslavia was or had been to its non-Serb inhabitants is open to debate, but it seems safe to say that while there were real causes for grievance, relatively small flames of resentment were fanned deliberately for political purposes.

In her powerful and disturbing collection of essays, *The Culture of Lies*[12] (translated into English in 1996), Dubravka Ugresic, born a Yugoslav but subsequently designated a Croat, describes how identity is created and manipulated for political ends. In one essay she writes of the different kinds of symbolic 'kitsch' used to foster identities based on the one hand on socialism and on the other hand on nationalism. She goes on to explain a more profound difference:

> The socialist state kitsch was created in peacetime, in a country with a future before it. This other kitsch, this 'gingerbread heart culture', is poured like icing over the appalling reality of war.

The wars in the Balkans have been referred to as 'The War Next Door'[13] but the war closest to home for British people, because it is (legally) *at* home, is the war in Northern Ireland. This one, too, was based on real grievances, but again it is hard to believe that they could not have been addressed equally productively in other ways, and without the horrible effects of sustained intercommunal violence.

Ironically, the UK government, while it was loudly endorsing the bombing of Serbia, was struggling to keep the Northern Ireland peace process on the road. In that case it had been decided that it was necessary, for the sake of all who live in Northern Ireland, to include 'the men of violence' in the dialogue and to draw them into the political processes aimed towards peace. This was a courageous decision, which has been vindicated by the slow and bumpy but nonetheless encouraging progress which has since been made – more so than many years of suppression.

Are there causes for which states might justifiably go to war against other states? Maybe the categories for intrastate wars offered by our original typology can help us here. The largely self-interest-based and greedy military activities described so far can be aligned with the 'factional' category. They are, however, often justified on ideological grounds and indeed it is hard and perhaps foolish to separate actions from the belief systems of those who promote and endorse them. The identity, autonomy and control category for internal wars is easily transferable to interstate wars. In law states have a right not to be interfered with and to defend their independence. This right is, however, being increasingly challenged and 'relativised' in practice, as recent wars have demonstrated – wars that have ostensibly been waged (among other reasons) to protect the rights of people within those countries.

Many would argue, conscientiously, that state boundaries should not be sacrosanct and that when terrible things are being done within them 'something should be done'. Current international law states that it is not acceptable for a state to take a decision to go to war against another state unless it has been invaded or is about to be attacked. That 'about to be' is in itself also relative and open to interpretation (and, as we have seen, to abuse). World War II was fought for security reasons, no doubt, but also for ideological reasons and to prevent the expansion of a regime that was objectionable on both practical and moral grounds.

Broadly speaking, then, we can say that there are just and unjust causes for which wars are fought and that they are often mixed. This brief review of the reasons for which wars in the past half-century have been launched suggests that vested interests of one sort or another have played a pre-eminent role. These are not the reasons that are given by politicians to their publics.

One final but important point before I move on to the motives of war leaders. Acts of terrorism may be an element in intrastate violence. They may also take on an international dimension and be directed at states from without as well as from within. Terrorism of this kind eludes our typology, and even our definition of war, but it is indeed a form of warfare that crosses state boundaries. Though it may be seen as factional, its motivations seem to be ideological as well as related to identity and a sense of outraged dignity.

Social anthropologists will tell us that dignity is a far stronger motivating factor in 'traditional' than in 'modern' cultures.[14] It is said that while Western identity is largely based on material things, others put far greater emphasis on respect and honour. Thinking back over the events of recent years I am convinced that we need to take this far more seriously.

WAR LEADERS AND THEIR MOTIVATIONS

Decisions to go to war are taken, in the last analysis, by political leaders and it is they who are most active in justifying those decisions. In 'The Birth of War' Brian Ferguson argues that elites exploit the fact that a strong sense of group identity encourages feelings of collective injury and a desire for collective retaliation, and go to war in pursuit of their own interests, often using people on the margins of society to fight for them. '[In] most cases – not every single one – the decision to wage war involves the pursuit of practical self-interest by those who actually make the decision … leaders often favour war because war favours leaders.' They really do lead us into war for their own reasons.

At the same time, leaders are not all-powerful and events have their own momentum. Historians have described, for instance, how, in the run-up to World War I, leaders were caught up in the sequence of events, sucked into and then trapped in the dynamic of war.[15] Sometimes they stitch themselves up by their own early choices and rhetoric and so stumble into war because they have left themselves with no (unembarrassing) way back. The presentation of causes and outcomes then follows – just as Tony Blair constantly reworked his arguments for supporting George Bush's war on Iraq in a desperate attempt to justify the unjustifiable. Much has been said about the relationship between George Bush Junior and his father, and the desire of one to complete the unfinished business of the other.

It seems clear that Tony Blair, once caught in a 'brotherhood' relationship with the US President, found it impossible to extricate himself from it, much as he might, eventually, have wished to. He would also have found it extremely difficult to step aside from his 'embattled man of principle' persona, other than by resigning his

position. It was clear from the start that the US was determined
to go to war and the military momentum would have been very
hard to counter (despite the anxiety of military leaders in the UK
about such a war's legality).

Leading their countries into war seems to have a bizarrely
positive effect on the popularity of leaders. Margaret Thatcher's
own popularity was restored by the Falklands War. In times
of crisis, people's need for security has to be projected on to
someone. Since those who may be responsible for the crisis are
also the only people who have the necessary power and authority,
they are, ironically, the ones relied on, and often qualities which
are unattractive in peacetime suddenly appear to be desirable
strengths.

To place oneself in such a role clearly appeals to those who
like to lead. Although it is perhaps too easy to impute motives
to others, it would appear that Tony Blair's love of his own
importance and of power alliances played a major role in his
decision to stick close to the US and its President, contrary to
the wishes of his own people and of his major European allies.
Righteous indignation is also a pleasant emotion and an external
enemy does wonders for the self-esteem, while at the same time,
as has often been observed, diverting attention from anything
unsatisfactory at home.

Thomas Merton argues that those who launch wars do so
because of a deep psychological attraction to it:

> [War] ... is a complete suspension of reason. This is at once
> its danger and the source of immense attraction ... the awful
> danger of war is not so much that force is used when reason
> has broken down but that reason unconsciously inhibits itself
> beforehand in order that it may break down and in order that
> resort to force may become inevitable.[16]

While I would not put all wars down to such deep and
overwhelming psychological attraction, I am persuaded that it
does play its part, in some cases at least.

I do not wish to suggest that people who lead their countries
into wars – even those that by common consent are the most
unnecessary ones – are more wicked or flawed than the rest of
us: only that they have achieved positions of power where their

weaknesses are dangerous. I believe that they persuade themselves of their own rightness – that they believe, to some extent at least, in the myth they perpetuate. No doubt they do have some certainty about the benefits which their hegemony can bestow.[17] Nor would I claim that they are fully aware of the falseness of their arguments. I have clear childhood memories of lying to my parents, and of the smarting indignation I felt when accused of dishonesty, and of the fresh arguments I brought to convince them and me. I take this to be a common human experience. But it has grave consequences when played out on the world stage.

The personal motivations and interactive chemistry of leaders can work for good as well as ill. It is said that the mutual liking between Ronald Reagan and Mikhail Gorbachev (and indeed between Mikhail Gorbachev and Margaret Thatcher), however unlikely, was instrumental in bringing about political détente. According to some, the fact that his son was nearing fighting age contributed to the decision made by the leader of the 'Tamil Tigers', Velupillai Prabhakaran, to call for a ceasefire in the Sri Lankan civil war. The personal interests of politicians, their career needs and their desire to cut an impressive figure in the world, as well as their convictions, capacities and judgement, play a vital role in the creation and unfolding of events.

While I think it is important to acknowledge that the personal thinking and behaviour of leaders can have a huge impact on events, I would not wish to suggest that they operate in a vacuum, wielding all the power and bearing all the responsibility. All those who work with them, advise them, support them, lobby them or fail to oppose them are complicit in what they do. And they operate within existing systems and cultures. I will explore these wider mechanisms and influences in Chapter 3.

'Humanitarian causes' for war are the most beguiling, but the evidence suggests that they are usually a cover for hegemonic interests and that where such interests are weak there will be little or no intervention. One does not need to be too cynical to conclude that in the broad sweep of history, decisions to go to war (whether civil or international) have not normally been governed by pure altruism or fought between 'goodies' and 'baddies'. Rather they have been the manifestations of rolling power contests between one potentate or one faction and another, with 'ordinary people' being dragged into the process as foot soldiers or caught up in the violence as civilian casualties.

There are issues of justice, human rights and self-determination that most of us would deem worthy of struggling for or defending and many situations in the world that – rightly – stir our indignation and compassion. These call for action. In most cases little or no action is taken by the outside world. Not long ago, for instance, Chris Patten, Europe's Commissioner for External Relations, was asked in a radio interview what should be done about Burma, where Aung San Suu Kyi had been detained incommunicado and without trial for her democratic activities and many of her followers killed. His response, effectively, was that we couldn't intervene in all the places where human rights violations and despotism were endemic.[18] The war in East Timor had gone on for decades before the 'international community' decided to intervene. Between 2000 and 2003 the war in the Congo has claimed 3 million lives while the world looked on – or away.

The question of what could and should be done in such situations will also be discussed in Chapter 5. Suffice it here to say that passivity and counter-violence are not the only options. There are countless situations, of every kind and at every level, that have been changed by social and political action. Sometimes that change has been achieved remarkably quickly and dramatically and at other times over a long period and in the face of many setbacks. But that is how most changes are brought about – including 'regime change'. Even the grasp of tyrants slips. Latin America, while still turbulent and scarred by poverty, nonetheless bears testimony to this. South Africa, too, where it was mass civil disobedience in the townships that had the greatest impact in overcoming apartheid. Although non-military and nonviolent alternatives of all kinds will be discussed later in the book, I will in the meantime illustrate the second of the false assumptions on which the war myth is based, by focusing on one case in which not even the most obvious alternatives were exhausted.

'EXHAUSTED ALTERNATIVES': THE CASE OF KOSOVO

As I argued in Chapter 1, the recent hegemonic wars on Afghanistan and Iraq were not waged for just causes, though they were presented as 'humanitarian wars'.[19] Nor were they launched as a last resort. But the case for them was fortified by constant references to the Kosovo War, cited as an example of the right use of military power. At the time, we were assured that it was a war of 'last resort'. For that reason it is key to debate in the West, a prime example of the war myth in action. Moreover, it is hard to refute the claim that 'everything else had been tried' – to prove a negative – other than by a detailed demonstration of the things that *could* have been tried in a particular case. For these two reasons I will address this question by taking the war on Kosovo as a case study and examining it in some detail. Though my main focus will be on what else could have been done, I will begin with a look at the validity of the war's proclaimed purpose and end with a review of its outcome.

This war, like its successors, was billed as a humanitarian war. The propaganda for it was skilful and, with few exceptions, little was done at the time, or has been since, to counter that propaganda. Those endless and terrible pictures of desperate human beings, old and young, trudging in terror along rough roads, to escape murder in their own apartments and villages, will long be etched on our memories. They will be remembered by most people as the cause of the NATO war on Serbia, rather than (as was actually the case) as one of its immediate effects. In fact, retired ministers and military men warned against the Kosovo War, predicting that the proposed NATO action would not prevent but rather trigger atrocities on a massive scale. Why, then, was it begun?

It would seem fair to suggest that the need to be seen to act was an overriding factor, after the opprobrium heaped upon the West for its laggardly response to the earlier wars in what had been Yugoslavia. Those were brought to an uneasy and unsatisfactory halt by the Dayton Agreement and, because Slobodan Milosevic was necessary to its achievement, he was confirmed by it in his position and the situation in Kosovo was left unaddressed. Milosevic's defiance of the West made his continuing role irksome not only because of his policy in relation to Kosovo but for wider political reasons. While dictators flourish in many parts of the world, to have such a man in power in Europe was not acceptable.

The oppression of the Albanian population in Kosovo was real and it was severe. It was easy (and right) to suggest that the situation was unacceptable and to make the case that there was just cause for some sort of intervention. However, to claim that this action was taken as a last resort was untrue, and was itself based on two false assumptions. The first was that everything else had been tried and the second that those other attempts had been proved conclusively to be without any hope of success or somehow rendered impossible to continue. In fact, very little had been done, and that belatedly, inadequately and disingenuously. Since this war has been given such a key role in justifying subsequent Western wars of 'intervention' (that word itself is loaded with assumptions), I will review the events which culminated in this NATO war and set out some of the actions which could have been taken at each stage to address the situation in other ways.

The crisis which culminated in the NATO bombing campaign, in death and destruction, and the expulsion of more than 1 million Albanians from their homes and land, had been building up over ten years and more. Slobodan Milosevic came to power at a time of major upheaval, after the collapse of Communism, when politics and identities were being redefined. Kosovo had, since 1974, been an autonomous or self-governing region within Yugoslavia. It was, however, impoverished, and most of the best jobs went to minority Serbs and Montenegrins. In the 1980s there was increasing unrest and in 1989 Milosevic used this situation to consolidate his political standing as a nationalist and champion of Serbs, rescinding Kosovo's autonomy. Step by step, Kosovo's independent institutions were closed down, Albanians were removed from all positions of power, and in total more than 70 per cent of Albanians were sacked from their jobs.

The response of the Albanian population of Kosovo, under the leadership of Ibrahim Rugova, was to launch a massive campaign of nonviolent resistance, setting up 'parallel institutions', opening their own schools and medical services. In addition, large public demonstrations were organised, though by the mid-1990s these public actions had diminished.[20]

What could have been done at this stage?

- Support at all levels for the nonviolence campaign; solidarity actions around the world; intergovernmental attention to human rights and development needs in Kosovo.

- Political and economic incentives for the Serbian government to restore the human rights of Albanians and other marginalised groups in Kosovo and to renegotiate the constitutional status of Kosovo.
- Dialogue at every level, including that of political leadership; exploration of new forms of political and constitutional relationship to overcome the impasse on sovereignty.
- Stronger links between peace and human rights activists in 'Serbia proper' and those in Kosovo.
- A consistent, regional approach in all negotiations and agreements related to the break-up of the former Yugoslavia.

The human rights abuses against the majority Albanian population and some non-Serb minorities, along with the parallel structures and other forms of resistance, continued in what had been Yugoslavia throughout the war, which began in 1991 and was formally ended by the Dayton Agreement in 1995. At the time of that agreement, no provision was made for addressing the conflict in Kosovo by restoring human rights and democracy there. Although, as we have seen, the power of Slobodan Milosevic, who was used by the Western powers to persuade Radovan Karadzic to sign the agreement, was consolidated by this tacit recognition, Serbia was subsequently made a 'pariah state' and punished economically and politically. With its own huge population of refugees from Croatia and Bosnia, and massive unemployment, Serbia was a beleaguered state, and the suffering of its people was intense. Despite the heroic efforts of peace and democracy movements in Serbia, human rights and democratic processes were constantly under attack, and the situation in Kosovo continued to deteriorate.

What could have been done at this stage?

- Incentives for democratisation and devolution in Serbia.
- Support for 'civil society' organisations in all parts of Serbia working for peace and democracy.
- Support for the continuing nonviolent movement in Kosovo.
- Dialogue between the nonviolent movement in Kosovo and the opposition movement in Serbia.

- Facilitation of inter-ethnic dialogue at the grass-roots level and among middle-level leaders.
- Economic and political incentives for all parties to reach a settlement.
- Respect and encouragement for Russia's potential intermediary role in persuading the Serb President to introduce reforms, rein in his police and allow the monitoring of human rights.
- A consistent, regional approach in all negotiations and agreements related to the break-up of the former Yugoslavia.
- Political action on the situation in Kosovo and negotiation for agreement over its future status alongside the Dayton Agreement.

As human rights abuses intensified, the nonviolent campaign and its leadership came under increasing pressure to abandon nonviolence in favour of armed struggle. Western failure to support Rugova and his followers created a situation in which Kosovar Albanians could argue that nonviolence had failed and conclude that only violence would win the attention they needed. In 1996 the Kosova Liberation Army (KLA) was formed, and fed into a spiral of violence in which murders of Serb police and militia by the KLA were countered by wholesale attacks on Albanians. After years of warnings and neglect, and as assaults on villages escalated, with many notorious atrocities, as well as smaller-scale acts of vengeance and intimidation, international attention was intensified. Permission was given by the Serb government for the introduction of an OSCE (Organization for Security and Co-operation in Europe) 'verification mission' of human rights monitors into Kosovo. Two thousand was the proposed number. In fact, fewer than 1,300 were sent, and most of those belatedly. Even this relatively small team of observers made a remarkable difference and, although there were still atrocities, they were far fewer in number. It seems reasonable, therefore, to believe that if the full number of monitors had been sent, and that if they had been well prepared for their task (rather than almost entirely unprepared) they could have gone a long way to ending the killings.

What could have been done at this stage?

- Sending in, quickly, the full complement of monitors, whether UN or OSCE, with appropriate backgrounds and training; providing them with expert advice and full logistical support, and allowing them to do their job.
- Creating a space for serious talks and negotiations at all levels, and concerted international support for a peaceful interim settlement of the conflict: a *modus vivendi* which would protect human rights, and a process for ongoing consideration of the constitutional issue.
- Giving authority to the UN to act as intermediary and using the 'good offices' of Russia.
- Making it clear that the issue was one of human rights, not of blanket hostility to Serbs or disregard for Serb perspectives.

Instead, the OSCE verification mission was abruptly withdrawn, deadlines were set, and in the Rambouillet 'talks' the 'international community' suddenly shifted its own position, placing the possibility of a constitutional separation on the table for the first time. This was done in order to induce the Albanian Kosovars to participate. It meant that Slobodan Milosevic was asked to accept, at 'gunpoint', radically new proposals for which his electorate was in no way prepared. When he refused to sign the proposed 'agreement', it was announced, without any UN debate, that there was no choice but for NATO to launch an attack.

There were no easy solutions to events in what was once Yugoslavia. We cannot say, 'If only this and this had been done, everything would have been all right.' We can, however, say that there were constructive things that could have been done, given the will and resources, and that mistakes were made at many stages, because of prevailing interests in the West, the lack of any coherent approach, the lack of respect for local populations, and the lack of any serious analysis of what the 'military solution' was likely to achieve. In this case as elsewhere, uncritical and ill-founded trust in what is euphemistically called 'force' was coupled with a lack of commitment to non-military action already well within the current scope of governments.

The level of effort that went into addressing the problems of
Kosovo by non-military means – that is, remarkably little effort – is
not unusual. It is typical. Where vested interests or public pressure
eventually demand some kind of action, the resort to military
'solutions' seems to be the chosen option. This means that the
potential repertoire of non-military responses remains massively
underdeveloped. War may be a way of defeating an enemy (if one
is the winner) but it is a very poor way of creating peace, as I will
argue now, as I address the third assumption of the war myth: that
war works, delivering good results for good causes.

WAR'S EFFICACY FOR GOOD

Let us look first at the outcome of NATO's war on Kosovo.

As various military experts warned, the violence against
Albanians in Kosovo was not stopped but massively increased,
and the terrible exodus began. Civilians of all ethnicities were
killed.

The infrastructure of Kosovo and of the rest of Serbia was
severely damaged, chemical pollution and the radiation from
depleted uranium in warheads poisoned the region, the land was
littered with deadly cluster bombs, and all hope of inter-ethnic
coexistence in Kosovo was propelled decades into the future. The
hatred engendered by what had been done by the Serb militias
and by NATO's action was such that the space for inter-ethnic
tolerance had been virtually eradicated. The Albanian population,
seeing its aspirations for separation as having been vindicated,
was no longer open to continuing within the same framework
as Serbia, but demanded full statehood. Ethnic minorities and
tolerant Albanians were intimidated and murdered.

Most Serbs were forced to flee and those who remained were
able to do so only under the protection of international forces,
unable to move outside their 'enclaves'.

How could it have been otherwise? After all, violence had been
upheld by international action, as their means of choice. How
could it be expected that when the 'international community'
had made Serbs the enemy the Albanian population of Kosovo
should not feel entitled to treat them in the same way? I was
present in Pristina when large and angry demonstrations were
taking place because some former KLA fighter had been brought

to court for crimes committed during the war or since. People were incensed. 'We were your allies in the war,' they said. 'Now our leaders are being treated like criminals.' Once again, war has apparently affirmed and amplified a kind of violent behaviour that has nothing to do with peace and its norms.

Meanwhile, local capacities for self-reliance have been seriously undermined by the overwhelming international presence, military and humanitarian, in Kosovo, which soaked up skilled personnel for menial work. The local economy, already weak, was destroyed, to be replaced by an elicit and exploitative 'black' economy. (It is ironic that those involved in illegal and immoral trading know no ethnic boundaries but work together most effectively.) The majority population is disillusioned and intimidated. Few dare to speak out against the new tyrannies of those who came to power through war, or of those who have used the social, political and economic hiatus it caused to set up their own nefarious empires. The territory is no nearer to democratic pluralism than it ever was and, like Bosnia, will look to armed forces to maintain its uneasy stability for years to come. Though the overall international presence is shrinking there, it is mainly because funds and personnel are being transferred to the newly devastated countries of Afghanistan and Iraq.

It was easy for NATO to say, as George Bush Junior did when he announced the end of major hostilities in Iraq, that 'we have prevailed'. But military victory (in both these cases against 'enemies' incapable of much military resistance) did not signal the accomplishment of the good things that were claimed as justification for war. Regime change was indeed brought about, but peace? An end to ethnic cleansing? Ethnic coexistence and plural democracy?

Were the effects of war in Kosovo an exception? What effects could be seen as justifying a war, if any? War is usually 'sold' to us, in one way or another, implicitly or explicitly, on the grounds that it will bring peace.[21] To discuss its efficacy in doing that we need a working definition. It is useful to divide it into two: 'negative peace'[22] or the absence of fighting, and 'positive peace'. I would define the latter as a state of affairs in which the people's human needs – physical and mental – are met; in which there is political freedom for all and a just share in power, responsibility and wealth; in which there is a culture of respect and care, reflected in laws, systems and behaviour, and in which there is a capacity to deal constructively with conflict. The 'security' reasons for war that have been under discussion correspond with the idea of 'negative peace' and the 'freeing people from dictatorship' reasons are related to the idea of 'positive peace'. How effective is war in these terms?

First, the military outcome of war – victory or defeat – which is the precondition for its efficacy along any lines, is hard to predict with certainty. It is dependent on the relative power to inflict damage by violence of one sort or another on the one hand, and the power to withstand that violence on the other, but many factors come into that equation. Hitler could have won World War II and millions of lives could have been sacrificed in vain. The introduction of new 'players' and other factors can shift the balance of power within the war dynamic. New and overwhelming weaponry may be introduced. While in some cases this may prove decisive, superior firepower may be more than matched by the tenacity of those who resist. Who could have foreseen the defeat of the US in Vietnam? (And I write at a time when parallels are beginning to be drawn between Vietnam and Iraq.)

Even if military victory is secured by those who claim to have gone to war for 'peaceful causes', what does war actually achieve in those terms? Let us look at the war whose 'effectiveness' is hardly ever questioned. The outcome of World War II is usually presented simply as 'Hitler and fascism were defeated', but the reality was far more complex. Terrible things had taken place and many of the war's consequences were unforeseen. Certainly Hitler was dead and the military victory of 'the Allies' prevented the creation of a fascist German Empire. But in the meantime 6 million Jews had been murdered in the death camps and across the world, in the global conflagration, 40 million people had died. The first atomic bombs had been developed and dropped on Hiroshima and Nagasaki and the Cold War and the arms race – conventional and nuclear – had begun in earnest. Eastern Europe and the Baltic states had been handed over to Russia and become part of the Soviet Empire. While world attention was elsewhere, Mao Tse Tung had triumphed and China too had come under communist control.

In the UK, among the unforeseen effects of the war were the weakening of class structures and the founding of the Welfare

State under a Labour government. But times were hard and the economy had been greatly weakened. It could no longer sustain the military capacity necessary for empire. Britain's power in the world was on the wane.

The damage inflicted on Germany had been terrible. Its infrastructure and economy took many years to repair. Japan, too, had suffered much damage. But with a ban on arms production in place and all their efforts put into technological research and development for civilian purposes, the economies of both Germany and Japan went from strength to strength and their industrial supremacy was assured.

In short, the impact of World War II was immense and beyond the control of those who fought it – even that of the victors. While it achieved the original, anti-expansionist objectives of the Allies, it was catastrophic in terms of human suffering. It unleashed new and terrible forces of violence, and while it halted one manifestation of tyranny it enabled the expansion of another.

To come back to the present and the impact of the War on Terror: since the war on Iraq there have been repeated public references to the difficulty of 'winning the peace', in contrast with the ease of 'winning the war'. This relative difficulty is hardly surprising. War is a process of destruction, in which brute force can achieve a great deal very quickly. But if it leaves people alive it also leaves alive the possibility of continuing opposition, so that even the security of the victor remains under threat and the local population lacks the safety needed for building peace.

Positive peace, which also needs security, implies the general wellbeing of a population (though this will always be relative). That, in turn, involves many things: economic provision; security to live your life without undue interference or threat; a say in the things that affect you; peace of mind; positive relationships with others; help when it is needed; education and a role in society, for instance. Despite the fact that wars may be waged with the proclaimed aim of achieving such 'humanitarian' goals, war has a catastrophic impact on all these things. British Foreign Secretary Jack Straw was right when he said recently in a discussion about Israel–Palestine, 'If people want peace, the only way of getting it is through a peace process.'

Whatever the gloss put on them, the fruits of the West's recent wars have in reality been like ashes in the mouth, having achieved

Dead Sea ashes

neither negative nor positive peace. How could it be otherwise? Through our actions we have violated all the principles of peace, democracy and international law. It is as if one could blast a huge crater where a 'regime' once was and then magically insert harmonious and democratic stability in its place. As if one could weave in a moment – or even in months – the necessary intricate webs of relationships and systems which need to be developed slowly, organically. As if one could bestow from above and from outside what should grow upwards, from within. As if one could expect people to welcome invasion by a 'liberator' who had brought their country low and contributed to the deaths of half a million and more of their children through sanctions, and respond by enacting values that have been crudely and massively violated in front of their very eyes.

Remember the US general who told reporters that looters in Basra were just reclaiming what was their own? Remember the crude jokes, the packs of cards and the lists for assassination, the smashing of statues? These were part and parcel of the culture of war – not of peace. No wonder the looting and lynching followed, and the destruction of a civilisation's history. What happened on the streets of Iraq's cities when all systems were destroyed or suspended was a frightening emblem of our need for order and of its fragility. The murder of one of the three women on the US-appointed Iraqi Council was emblematic of the triumph of machismo over humanity. The hold of the new mafia in Kosovo is another such example. To transform an ugly dictatorship into a free and just society is indeed a worthy aspiration, but to try to do so by crude, ignorant and dictatorial violence is to show a very poor grasp of the nature of freedom or justice or society.

Wars are made up of acts of enmity rather than co-operation, of imposition rather than negotiation, of summary killing rather than due process, of destruction rather than creation. Peace (positive peace), by my definition, is a state in which the culture of the people, the structures within which they live, the relationships between them, and the attitudes and behaviours which they display are characterised by mutual respect. If this is a fair description, trying to achieve peace by war is, to use a well-known metaphor, like trying to grow figs from thistles.[23]

Moreover, one form of violence overwhelmed by another is likely to reappear in a new form, so that even negative peace remains under threat. To put one's faith in war as a means of achieving a more ordered world is to ignore the fundamental lawlessness of having a world controlled by armed and economic might. It is to accept the use of naked aggressive power to achieve dominance. Law, by contrast, is designed to regulate the use of power. The laws of war may seek to curb it, but the logic of war brooks no limits. Restraint may be exercised when it can be afforded, but the victory imperative is the ultimate driving force.

Because of its overwhelming military power, the US is currently able to ignore all the international institutions designed to regulate international behaviour. The world's 'international policeman' does not support international law. Having attempted to subvert the UN by bribing and bullying Security Council members, it was then able to ignore it.[24] And, unsurprisingly, the US refuses to make itself answerable to the International Court. It will not be held accountable by any Hague Tribunal. Indeed, the laws of war have until now brought only the defeated to justice – never the victors. A system where war is seen as the ultimate arbiter is by its very nature incompatible with the rule of law and international agreements through the UN. In such a system no nation that has the power to 'call the shots' militarily will give up its power to do so, putting itself on a level with those that do not.

The terribly reasonable-sounding head of the UK mission in Iraq said recently, 'We've got an opportunity to settle this region', thus exposing the whole arrogant and mistaken theory that peace can be imposed from outside by war. The war dynamic constricts and displaces constructive and co-operative forms of action, forcing them into the margins or leaving those who promote them to pick up the pieces that war has created. Peace anywhere must be made by the people who live there. Wars issue at best in the imposition of 'peace' by the victors on the vanquished or in a deal struck between different warring parties in which the wishes of those who did not fight are ignored.

To put one's faith in war to achieve human rights is equally contradictory. War is made up of human rights violations. It is based on a fundamental division between 'us' and 'them', which makes human rights – based on fundamental equality – a nonsense. Even the notion of the protection of 'innocent civilians' (as against soldiers, who are therefore by implication guilty) has nothing to do with human rights, which do not depend on innocence and guilt, but are unconditional. Whatever the rules of war, and notwithstanding the outcry at the alleged 'execution' of British soldiers in Iraq, in essence the killings which it entails are all a form of execution without trial. 'Operation decapitation' and the list of those wanted 'dead or alive' constituted what Arundhati Roy called 'the most elaborate assassination attempt in history'[25] – though live enemies can talk while dead ones cannot, so many on the 'wanted' list were in practice taken prisoner rather than killed.

The treatment of the prisoners held at the US base in Guantanamo Bay – some of them children – has shocked all those concerned for civil liberties and the legislation supporting them. But the overwhelming military power of the US, which enables it to impose its will around the world, allows it also to contravene international norms unscathed. Meanwhile, the War on Terror has seen civil liberties diminished in many countries, including the UK. To put one's country on a 'war footing' is to claim the right to restrict freedom of movement and information, and to create a climate in which measures which would otherwise seem unthinkable are seen as justified. The Spanish government even introduced legislation creating an offence of 'defeatism' to control freedom of expression in opposition to war. And while we concentrate on control, we fail to build the bridges that really could enhance our safety.

The US attacks on Al Jazeera's office in Kabul and later in Bagdhad (as well as the hotel where the international press corps were staying), like the bombing of the TV station in Serbia, were a clear expression of the hostility of war leaders to the democratic principle of freedom of expression and information. Propaganda is an instrument of war – bad when it comes from 'them', but called 'news' when it comes from 'us'.

In a democracy, decisions are made through dialogue and an agreed process. Democracy cannot be imposed – only practised. It may be supported, encouraged and learned by example. War contradicts its most fundamental principles. Even when sincere attempts have been made (as I believe they have in Kosovo) to support its establishment, a contrary example has been given, and the dynamics and values of war persist and are inimical to it.

Democracy also implies open government. But just as deception is an instrument of war,[26] war leaders deceive their publics about the realities they face. They have every reason to keep their public and their allies with them by putting a positive gloss on things. So at the moment there are attempts in the US to keep to a minimum television footage on the daily killings of US troops in Iraq and fake letters purporting to come from US soldiers have appeared in local newspapers, claiming to represent a high level of determination and optimism. War leaders also stoop to more blatant forms of public deception in justifying their actions – such as Tony Blair's 'dossier' of 'evidence' against Saddam Hussein, famously containing (doctored and without acknowledgement) an out-of-date PhD thesis.

But surely wars *can* have good results? Resisting invasion and removing tyrants are good purposes that can be achieved by war, are they not? And surely there are cases where it is criminal not to intervene? There are two things at issue here, I think. The first is the inadequacy of war to address complex and entrenched situations of intense violence – such as that in the Congo – even if the will existed to do so, which it does not. The second is the cost of wars fought for 'just causes' – even when those causes are genuine. The costs are not only those suffered by affected populations but, as with the wars already referred to, the costs of violating and contradicting the humane values for which such wars are fought which in turn affect the conduct of these wars and the cruelty they involve. They are costs that are incorporated in the outcome of such wars, the effects of widespread violence on the successor society. Furthermore, unless the war power of those who set off to bring justice is greater than that of those they oppose, their war will bring only further repression or years of attrition. Whatever the stakes and the risks, such wars carry with them all the dire effects of other wars. Those are the only war outcomes that can be relied on.

THE NEGATIVE EFFECTS OF WAR

What we are never promised when a war is in the offing are its certain outcomes – effects that are contrary to the goal of peace and violate all of its values. While military outcomes may be uncertain, the havoc wreaked by war is predictable. Whatever its causes, its cost is immense. Its story throughout the ages has been one of the untold suffering of combatants and non-combatants alike, in which outcomes are decided by a combination of luck and power; a story in which even victories involve huge losses, misery and destruction. In the words of an email sent to me by a Serb friend, 'To the victors goes the prize and the prize is a heap of ashes.' It is a rather commonplace thought that if aliens were to visit our planet they would be incredulous at the destructiveness of our behaviour. Yet we do not carry this perspective into a serious reassessment of war as an institution.

Maybe one of the reasons we do not radically review the realities of war is that those realities are unbearable to contemplate and almost impossible to imagine. While the war on Iraq was still being threatened, our small grandchild burned his hand on a stove. His parents were distraught and his agonised screams, which went on for two hours, reduced us all to tears and near-collapse. This was no more than a superficial burn. A shot of morphine and an impressive bandage restored him and us to a shaken cheerfulness. But I was haunted by this brief insight into the intensity of suffering and have been confronted by this small event with the true enormity of the pain and anguish involved in war, in which there is, all too often, no morphine and no bandages, and those who escape injury and death are forced to watch helplessly the suffering of those around them.

The kinds of injuries caused in 'outrages' (rightly so named) like the destruction of the World Trade Center or the Bali bombing are graphically presented to us and are a matter of unbelieving horror. Somehow it is not clear that just such injury and death are commonplace in the wars waged by those somehow excluded from the 'axis of evil'.

But what of the terrible scenes described by Iraqi doctors working in looted hospitals without water or medicines? Or what of the man pictured on the front page of the *Jordan Times* in April 2003 – a man in Hillah, south of Baghdad, throwing up his arms to the sky in a gesture of grief. At his feet are the coffins of his three children, one an infant less than one year old. The man says he lost 15 members of his family when the pickup truck they were in was blown up by a rocket fired from an American Apache helicopter.

As I stood in a vigil during that war, a passer-by shouted, 'But the man was a mass murderer!' He did not wait for me to say to him that 'we' had also been mass murderers. When the war was over, some commentators argued that those who had opposed it should have changed their minds – as if the things to which we had said 'Not in my name' were things which we would now feel fine about. A friend made a new placard with a photograph of the sadly famous Iraqi child who lost both his arms, much of his skin and 15 of his relatives. Under the photograph he wrote the caption, 'Was this done in your name?' Once a war is over those far away who were its victims are rapidly forgotten. Having no voice to speak for themselves, those who have been 'liberated' by death, or relegated to the unseen ranks of the injured-dependent, no longer figure in the story. And those of us who live in safe places carry on with our lives as if nothing had happened.

While the recent wars of Western intervention are very much on my mind as I write, all wars, past and present, have terrible costs, whatever their proclaimed cause. World War II cost an unimaginable 40 million lives, with vast numbers incinerated or blown apart.

Although those who bear the brunt of war are mostly civilians, the misery of soldiers is not to be forgotten. Who could fail to pity the young men currently patrolling the streets and roads of Iraq, forbidden to speak to reporters of their low morale but waiting at any moment to be in the next jeep to be blown up or the next helicopter to be shot down. Those who eventually return home will do so with their minds scarred by what they have done and witnessed. Five times the number of soldiers who lost their lives in the last Gulf War have since committed suicide.[27]

Civil wars, guerrilla fighting and terrorism also have a terrible impact on the lives of those who endure them. Generations of young people 'give' their lives in them and take the lives of many more. While murderous insecurity holds sway, the poverty and deprivation that so often underlie such conflict remain. Much-needed development, even if the political will for it existed, is rendered impossible or constantly reversed. Breadwinners are away fighting; many are killed or incapacitated. Women are often left to cope with all the provision and care for children and older relatives in the harshest possible circumstances. A whole society is brutalised and the carnage leaves scars for generations.

Among the brutalities of war is the sexual violence that takes place within it. It does not happen under cover of war. The relationship is fundamental, not incidental, and overt rather than covert. Sexual violence is in itself an act of war. It is carried out against children and men as well as women, but women are its most frequent victims. It is more than an act of uncontained lust and brutality. Through sexual violence against women, men from one community 'prove' their masculinity and sexual superiority over their enemies. While sexual violence in war has received more attention in recent years than in the past (for instance, in relation to the war in Bosnia) and rape is now designated a war crime, the humiliation and abuse of women remain integral to the nature and conduct of war. In my next chapter I shall argue that understanding the connection between gender and war is vital to the liberation of human beings from the pernicious effects of both.

Immediate violence, injury and death are not, of course, the only ravages of war. The destruction of infrastructure takes a massive toll. When bombs are used, the killing is accompanied or followed by the destruction of homes, roads, bridges, factories, food stores, power plants, water supplies and so on (as was seen in Iraq). The loss of these facilities brings further suffering and death – sometimes on a huge scale. Their effects may reach well beyond a country's own borders. For instance, the bombing of Serb bridges over the Danube caused economic privations to several countries through which it flowed.

Often huge numbers of those affected by the threat and the effects of war flee their homes, forced to abandon their crops and any other means of livelihood, undertaking desperate journeys to unknown destinations – where life is a continuing nightmare. Quite commonly they are never able to return but have to rebuild their lives as best they can in dire circumstances, since the countries to which they are able to flee are extremely poor and those which could better afford to receive them are extremely inhospitable.

At a time when the protection of the earth and its creatures is such an urgent concern, the environmental impact of war seems to go almost unnoticed. While our planet has a miraculous capacity for regeneration, the destruction of animal life and the pollution of land and water occasioned by modern warfare should, in themselves, be a cause for profound concern. In the words of a friend,[28] 'War is the worst pollutant.' This may sound like an overstatement, but consider the burning of oil wells (in the Gulf), the removal of vegetation (in Vietnam) and killing of wildlife, the litter of destroyed machinery, the pollution of water supplies. In one day in Pancevo in April 1999, NATO bombs demolished a refinery, a fertiliser plant and an American-built petrochemical complex. This was one episode in 78 days of aerial assaults which caused environmental disasters across Serbia.

The daily, relentless pollution caused by military aircraft and land vehicles and by military production is less dramatic but cumulatively immense. The creation, storage and transport of 'weapons of mass destruction' (and indeed all modern weapons of war), let alone their use, constitute a threat to our environment, at a time when we are becoming frighteningly aware of our impact on it.

Some forms of war pollution have a directly catastrophic impact on human beings. Agent Orange, the defoliant used by the US in Vietnam, has caused (and continues to cause) terrible cancers and birth deformities. The depleted uranium used to harden warheads fired on Iraq in 1991 has had similar horrific consequences which have been well documented. But no one has been held accountable. And in spite of the limited success of international campaigning, landmines and cluster bombs have rendered much land unusable and continue to shatter limbs and destroy lives.

Any reckoning of the true cost of war must take into account not only the destruction and misery caused directly, but the resources of every kind which are needed to rebuild broken countries. A mere glance at TV footage of Afghanistan or Chechnya, for example, would give some sense of the size of the task that must lie ahead. And, soaring above all costs of reconstruction, is the cost of war itself: of the hardware and human resources used to wreak such havoc.

The obscene number of billions of pounds and dollars reportedly set aside for the war on Iraq represents vast wealth that could have been used to meet human need rather than destroy human life. (Of course arms manufacturers will have grown fat on the profits, but that is another matter.) There is never, it seems, any difficulty in funding war: money is no object. The US 'defence' budget recently went up by 25 per cent and the war on Iraq cost the US four times its annual aid budget.[29] But when it comes to reconstruction, or even funding regular, essential, domestic services, money always seems to be in short supply. In the words of US President Dwight D. Eisenhower:

> Every gun that is made, every warship that is launched, every rocket that is fired, signifies in the final sense a theft from those who hunger and are not fed, those who are cold and are not clothed.

Such a theft is an absolute denial of the justice and respect that must be at the heart of positive peace.

CONCLUSION

I am not arguing that there can never be good motives for war. I am arguing that wars are more often than not fought for reasons of self-interest, not altruism, and are 'won' by those who have the power to prevail rather than by those who are right. I am not arguing that there are no situations where there have seemed to be no alternatives to war. I *am* arguing that alternatives are often not tried and never exhausted. I am not arguing that war can achieve nothing positive. I *am* arguing that it is an unpredictable, high-risk strategy, whose certain bad effects are incalculable and whose capacity for delivering 'positive peace' is, in the local view, poor, and in the global sense nil. Even 'negative peace' is unlikely to be reached through the violation of the security of others.

Wars revive and entrench old enmities. Their half-life endures for generations. It is hard to imagine that the wars in the Balkans have made future wars there less likely. And I doubt whether many of us feel safer from terrorism because of the War on Terror. (Apparently Tony Blair had been warned by his intelligence officers that a war on Iraq would make the UK more rather than less likely to suffer terrorist attacks.) In terms of security, what the US's 'for us or against us' approach has achieved is to intensify the polarisation and hostility out of which the terrorism came. It has reinforced reactionary movements that win their support from those who feel humiliated, disregarded and impotent. War used to achieve negative peace is often only the prelude to long-term military control to keep a resurgence of violence at bay.

The cruelty and carnage of terrorist attacks speak for themselves. No doubt the likes of Osama bin Laden, like other war leaders, have mixed motives for what they do, but there is certainly no reason to suppose that they are, in contrast to their methods, somehow pure. Their democratic remit is nil. But those who, to whatever degree, support them do so out of a sense that this is the only way of getting back at those they see as global tyrants who disregard their needs, their dignity and their identity. In this sense, Peter Ustinov was right in saying that 'Terrorism is the war of the poor, and war is the terrorism of the rich'. War is the archetype of violence; terrorism is its poor relation. War provides the 'justification' for terrorism. But, unlike regular armies, terrorism can never be vanquished, only the support for terror removed by addressing its causes.

The Prime Minister of New Zealand, Helen Clark, discussing the conduct of the War on Terror and noting the size, population and economic growth of China, recently argued that Britain and the US might live to regret the unleashing of 'the law of the jungle' in international affairs. As she said, agreed and observed codes of international conduct were vital if weaker nations were not to be at the mercy of the most powerful.[30]

No past empires have proved indestructible and it seems foolish to think that the 'full spectrum dominance' of the US will be achievable or lasting. The 11 September attacks symbolised (as clearly they were intended to) the vulnerability of even the most powerful nation on earth, its vast war capability notwithstanding. At the moment the security of the West seems very tenuous, despite its massive firepower. Those of us who remember the 1960s will know how impermanent everything seemed then, including life itself and the future of our planet. Nothing fundamental has changed since then. The threat from nuclear weapons remains as great as ever – indeed it is greater, since those weapons have proliferated, as those of us who opposed them said they would. A world bristling with such potential for its own destruction, whose only 'stability' depends on the threat of the release of that potential, is a fragile world indeed. War as a 'last resort' could give 'lastness' a new and final meaning.

In the meantime, war as an institution continues to prove the enemy of any kind of positive peace and is disastrous for human beings and the planet. There is a ready supply of arms for those who wish to maintain control over restless populations, or to build their own wealth and power through military intimidation and war – just as the West has built its own power and continues to maintain it. Civil wars continue to ravage large parts of the world, particularly Africa and South East Asia. Most countries are marked by a cruel gulf between rich and poor – a gulf dividing every nation and defining the relationship between the North and West on the one hand and the South and East on the other. Development (what I would rather call the increase of human wellbeing) is hindered by war, by the economic dominance of the West, maintained by military dominance, and by the wealthy few within those societies who support their own positions through similar means. The earth is ravaged by wars and by the profligate consumption they are waged to protect.

Terrorism is part of the war dynamic, whatever the justifications made for it or the desperation of some of those who resort to it. While it may be impossible to eradicate, there is little to suggest that it does anything more than destroy lives, harden opposition and deepen hatred. 'Liberation wars' may be fought for valid causes, but bring in their wake great suffering. 'Insurgents' and government fighters are killed, along with the civilians caught up in their contest. Villagers see their animals taken to feed those who claim to represent them and 'collaborators' are tortured and killed. The fighting can be protracted over decades and more often than not achieves little if anything that could not have been achieved by other means.

Wars can accomplish certain negative things – the destruction of this or the removal of that – and there are undoubtedly things that should be destroyed or removed. But even the world's richest and most militarised nations are incapable of imposing their will on the entire world through military action – even if that will could be trusted, which it clearly cannot. And if they could, the result would be a new kind of tyranny, in which the power and responsibility of local populations were usurped by outsiders and in which they saw their cultures and histories swept aside.

War, by its very nature, embodies the tyranny that it claims to address. It is rarely waged for good reasons and in all cases produces unacceptable suffering. It is used before other means have been adequately tried, and those other means do exist, as I shall show in Chapter 5.

The worst effect of any war, even more terrible than the immediate outrages it involves, is that it destroys the ground of peace, erodes its culture and wrecks its institutions, so preparing the way for new wars, new suffering and the seemingly endless process of wrecking lives and squandering resources.

For us to live together in any kind of safety or to meet the real needs of human beings, like eliminating poverty or dealing with disease, the eradication of war is a prerequisite. And war is a very bad way of establishing the values that we claim to uphold, such as human rights, tolerance, understanding, forgiveness, co-operation or the rule of law. The myth of war as purely motivated and as the necessary and effective means of achieving anything humane must be dispelled once and for all.

3
War, Violence and Human Nature

Thou must be patient; we came crying hither:
Thou know'st the first time that we smell the air
We waul and cry.

William Shakespeare, *King Lear*

Man, proud man, drest in a little brief authority, most ignorant
of what he's most assured, his glassy essence, like an angry
ape, plays such fantastic tricks before high heaven, as makes
the angels weep.

William Shakespeare, *Measure for Measure*

The soul that rises with us, our life's Star,
Hath had elsewhere its setting
And cometh from afar:
Not in entire forgetfulness,
And not in utter nakedness,
But trailing clouds of glory do we come
From God, who is our home

William Wordsworth, *Intimations of Immortality*

We conclude that biology does not condemn humanity to war,
and that humanity can be freed from the bondage of biological
pessimism ... Just as wars begin in the minds of men [sic],
peace also begins in our minds. The same species who invented
war is capable of inventing peace. The responsibility lies with
each one of us.

Unesco, *Seville statement on violence*, 1989

In my work as a professional peace worker and an activist, I meet
a great many people who base their belief in war's inevitability
not only on the myth discussed in the last chapter but also on
the idea that human beings are doomed by their very nature to
destroy each other. In this chapter I want to discuss the question

of war and human nature and present a different view of where war comes from. I will start with a look at power.

POWER AS DOMINATION

What kind of power is used in war? Military power, evidently; but the weapons and strategies of war are the means of exercising power within a particular model: the model of domination[1] – of control or conquest *over* the other. It is not the only model available, as I shall discuss later, but more often than not, this is the one that springs to mind when we hear the word 'power'.[2] That is why we are often uncomfortable with the very idea of power and powerfulness. While we may secretly enjoy this kind of power, we are unlikely to admit it. Power has a bad press.

In this model, power is achieved by one individual or group over another to get the better of them. Essentially, it is about working against them. It need not always be enforced by violent means, but it is founded on the power and willingness to overpower others, against their will; to enforce one's will against theirs. It assumes a 'win–lose' relationship (either we must win and you must lose or vice versa). Typically, such relationships are maintained by violence or the threat of it. They infringe the autonomy of the party that is dominated.

When we think of violence, we usually have in mind behaviour of a kind calculated to harm others, whether psychologically or physically. This can be done by attack of some kind – for instance, frightening, hurting, insulting, humiliating, striking, maiming or killing. But it can also include deprivation of what is necessary to human wellbeing: imprisonment or other deprivation of liberty or liberties; deprivation of food, water or medical help, or wider economic deprivation; or the denial of the opportunity to express one's fundamental values and identity.

VIOLENT STRUCTURES

While violent behaviour – direct violence – is the form of violence most easily identified, such visible infringements of basic human needs are supported by violent 'structures':[3] that is, by organisations and systems that inflict harm on people – and on other inhabitants of our planet, and indeed on the planet itself.

Military systems and organisations constitute one such structure. They perpetuate the capacity to deliver direct violence against those who threaten or compete with the interests of those who control them. Through this military capacity and its personnel and mechanisms, economic and political systems that violate the rights and needs of others are enforced.

Our system of states is predicated on violence, since a state is (with the single exception of Costa Rica) almost by definition a territory defended by the armed forces controlled by its government. Military violence is currently the means for imposing Western hegemony on the rest of the world and in the past it was the means to build and extend European and other empires. It was also used, eventually, to bring about their overthrow. It has ensured that violence is built into whatever has replaced them.

Armed violence is also the means of controlling oppressed populations within their own country, constituting a form of low-intensity warfare against them. If people rise up against cruelty and injustice in the system of control within which they are forced to live, their opposition is crushed by the violence of the state, or by private armies or company militias. And the poor are hired as foot soldiers in the military enforcement system.

Oppressed people also take up violence to try to overthrow those who have control over them and abuse them, thus entering into the violent dynamic in an active rather than a passive way.

By contrast, democracy is governance 'by the people and for the people', or at least by their consent. Yet most states that identify themselves as democratic see their armies as the final guarantee of their government's control. And ironically it is the countries that see themselves as the most democratic that most often use military violence against other states, to impose their wishes and uphold their interests.

In a triad of economic, political and military violence, it is hard to choose between the three, in terms of their power to inflict misery on human beings. In practice, they are inseparable.

The use and impact of military violence have been discussed in Chapter 2. Economic violence is the use of existing economic dominance, linked to political power and backed by military might, to subjugate the economic labour and systems of others and thereby exploit them. In itself it causes far more deaths than war, and arguably far more misery. It is the means by which most human deprivation is inflicted. But military violence is what keeps it in place, adding its own toll of suffering and impoverishment.

It has been argued that economics is a descriptive science, having in itself no moral content but merely identifying the way things work. But economists do make prescriptions, and once we have been helped by economic analysis to understand how wealth is created and controlled, we surely have a moral obligation to act on that understanding.[4] Just as wars do not hit us like meteorites but are started by people, economic activity does not happen to human beings but is undertaken by them, within frameworks of their design. In this economic realm of human activity and structures, some use their relative power, with the backing of armed violence, to control or exploit others.

While some do so illegally and are termed 'mafiosi' or 'gangsters', the most powerful do so within systems that condone, support and enable them. Not only are they backed by the military structures – they also grow rich by producing and selling the goods consumed by the military, whether official or unofficial. The irony is that big business supplies not only the arms that are used to protect it and extend its power but also those that are used to oppose it. Greed and grievance both feed the arms industry. The term 'military industrial complex' was well coined.[5]

There is growing disquiet that transnational corporations are encroaching on the territory of political decision-makers, and therefore eroding democracy. It may well be that the power of money is indeed curtailing democratic choice, since national income and the success of a country's economy are essential ingredients for political success. Transnational corporations have annual turnovers well in excess of the 'gross national products' of smaller and poorer countries. The economic interests may therefore find themselves in a position to dictate terms to politicians.

Politicians may be 'bought' as well as leaned on. Indeed, they may be hand in glove with the economic barons. The tendency for dictators to acquire vast personal wealth is well known. The vested interests of 'democratic' politicians and the gains they make through office, while not entirely hidden, deserve more attention. (For instance, George Bush and many members of his administration are closely linked with the arms and oil magnates of their country.)[6]

'Modern democracies' have all too often given military support to the most ugly dictatorships in order to further their own strategic and economic interests. They have been involved in 'destabilising' regimes and opposing or removing leaders inimical to their interests. The US, because of its 'need' to secure oil supplies to feed its vast and growing consumption, was heavily involved in Angola's long civil war and the history of its involvement in the Middle East is notorious. Britain and other European countries also have an inglorious history of interference in many countries.

In a recent report,[7] Christian Aid showed how the presence of oil and other mineral wealth in the countries of the 'developing' world has led not to increased wealth and development, but to the corruption of those in power, to massive military spending, and to the further impoverishment of ordinary people.

Such exploitation and abuse of power were formerly, in the West at least, of concern only to a politically aware and (to 'ordinary' people) somewhat suspect minority. Recent global events and the US rhetoric of 'full spectrum dominance' and its clear will to use its overwhelming military power to pursue it have, however, pushed these issues to the forefront of public awareness. The world is now described as 'unipolar', as if US control was now complete.

However, 'structures', though so described, are not fixed. The systems and relationships we are considering here are not only complex but dynamic. They are constantly shifting and changing. The whole global 'system' of capitalism is in reality a myriad of organisations, laws, people, activities, materials, transactions, communications and perceptions. It is not possible that all these elements, along with other unpredictables, such as the weather, or events not susceptible to systems (like the flying of aeroplanes into strategically important buildings), could combine in any fixed or stable way, or be controlled by anyone. If we think historically, the mutability of human systems is plain to see.

Arundhati Roy[8] describes the effects of 'structural adjustment' in India: a programme of privatisation and 'labour reforms' creating widespread loss of livelihoods and great misery. She says, 'While the elite journeys to its imaginary destination somewhere near the top of the world, the dispossessed are spiralling downwards into crime and chaos.' This is not stability. To counter the growing discontent which poverty has engendered, the Indian government sought to divide the poor against each other through crude Hindu nationalism as a diversion, colluding at atrocities terrible both in their nature and their scale. These terrible human rights abuses have been ignored by the West, because India has opened its market to global investors. The stranglehold of the economic power and military control may be tight, but this cannot be seen as a stable – still less a desirable – situation.

US AND THEM

In Chapter 2 I argued that one of the essential elements in war, which acts as a quasi-moral justification for it, is the separation of 'us' from 'them'. The same dichotomy is central to the dominatory model of power more broadly, since this kind of power is about control in the face of contest, about winners and losers, about controllers and controlled.

At the personal level, being a winner or loser may be influenced by such things as looks, money, education or position. At the group level, power relations are organised along several different lines: class or caste, tribe, clan, 'ethnic' group or religion (also gender, but more of that later). These divisions may or may not be enforced by law, but even when they are not, their effect all to often remains. In India and Sri Lanka, where the caste system has been outlawed, it still has a stranglehold on the lives of millions. In a BBC Radio interview, a former Republican Governor of Illinois, George Ryan, talking about the law as an instrument of justice, remarked, 'If you're poor and minority in our country you stand very little chance.'[9]

The archetype of separation is apartheid ('apart-hood'). Although the regime in South Africa has changed and the very notion of 'race' has been widely discredited, the injustice and violence surrounding 'racism' have not been magically removed from history or eradicated from present human relationships and structures. The categorisation of fellow human beings as inferior or subhuman was used to justify the most appalling atrocities, on a scale we now find hard to imagine[10] – given that they were committed not in an instant, by bombs, but by slower and more 'labour-intensive' means.

These racist wars of the past, and the consequent rape of whole continents and their resources, have left an ugly legacy. In the power structures and dynamics of the present, the former colonisers still hold economic, political and military sway over those they colonised, while racist attitudes and actions continue at the social and political level, engendering resentment and hatred.

The term 'global apartheid' was coined[11] to express the analysis that the separation of races in a particular context is a microcosm of the larger separation between rich and poor, which in global terms is one between the West and 'the rest'. Attempts to control population movement are designed not simply to make life manageable but to maintain that separation.

Gross disparities between rich and poor, like racism and other forms of 'us–them' oppression, are not the prerogative of the West. Abuse and cruelty are embedded in the cultures and structures of other societies and cannot all be attributed to the effects of colonialism. Sexism, inter-group violence and occult practices have far deeper roots. But through their own lust for dominance and their technological and military prowess, Western countries obtained such a grip on the resources, politics and economies of the Southern hemisphere that they are still able to maintain the dominant position that gives them such ongoing power for oppression. And the military back-up for that dominance is never wanting.

In most parts of the world, the wars on Afghanistan and Iraq were seen as racist wars, and in turn they have encouraged racist attitudes towards the 'Western powers'. This is the pernicious dynamic of an us–them power system. The losers suffer and the winners live in constant danger of retribution or reversal.

So US citizens live in fear of reprisals, just as others live in fear of attack by the US. Meanwhile, the US government sees new threats to its control. For instance, a new programme of co-operation between the US and India has been launched to 'contain' China (under Clinton regarded as a 'strategic partner' but under Bush as a 'strategic competitor') whose own approach recently had been more conciliatory than aggressive. The cost to India, a country with huge problems of malnutrition and illiteracy, will be a steep rise in its already damaging 'defence' bill. Its relations with China will become more rather than less tense. At the same time the likelihood of any US–Chinese partnership will be made more remote.

The cost of maintaining control over empires is immense and eventually leads to their collapse or dissolution.[12] This holds true for the whole project of domination, in whatever sphere. In the endless win–lose struggle, a great deal of energy goes into the maintenance of control and great harm is done.

It is remarkable and significant that the benefits of competition are so regularly extolled when we see its costs in every realm, from domestic to international. As in war, the casualties of the win–lose system do not always survive to tell their story. Equally, the diverted energy, wasted resources, lack of synergy and lost creativity are invisible.

VIOLENCE AND HUMAN NATURE

Surely, though, it is part of human nature to identify with some groups and against others, and to compete, fight? Selfishness and aggression have, it is argued, brought us where we are as a species.[13] Therefore we are doomed to continue along the same lines and to think otherwise is to delude ourselves.

If so, the outlook is grim for most of the world's population – and indeed for us all, since we are destroying our planet's capacity to sustain us and in any case are heading towards our own extinction, sooner or later, through some 'WMD' catastrophe. The human species would not be the first to have disappeared.

But surely such a gloomy 'determinist' view overlooks the other aspects of human nature which prompt us to behave altruistically, to care and be kind, to co-operate for our own benefit and that of others? It is not only our aggressive propensities that are inherent but our moral sense, too.[14] While we look back on centuries of war and cruelty, we are also capable of love, courage and dedication. We have the moral resources inherent in our humanity: altruism, respect, compassion, and the desire to be seen – by ourselves and others – to have done right. These human resources can provide the basis for curbing and transforming our destructive capacities. We have, alas, created circumstances in which our moral resources are often blocked and depleted, and in which it is all too easy to fall into the dynamics of violence. But those circumstances can be changed.

Determinism ignores our evolved capacity to think, understand and choose. Other animals adjust their behaviour, however instinctive, to meet new circumstances. They adapt – sometimes quite radically – in order to survive. It would be sad if we, with our large brains, could not do likewise. The greater our level of awareness, the greater our ability to choose. When my grandson is able to tell his parents that he is filling his nappy, he is ready to make the choice to use his pot instead. For good or ill, our thinking, decision-making and action will shape our future, which is not a fixed end, but a process that unfolds according to the choices we make. In the vast sweeps of described history, the motivations and choices of real human beings are lost from view. But each one of us, whether actively or passively, positively or negatively, will contribute in however small a way to the unfolding of the human story.

Not only do we as individuals experience choice: we see those around us acting altruistically as well as selfishly, constructively as well as destructively, wisely as well as foolishly. And we see people change as a result of experiences they undergo, people they meet and things they read. It is true that individual human beings are also part of a larger reality, not separate from it. But the fact of human agency remains. We contribute to the ongoing stream of reality. And the choices that we make are not determined by our biological and psychological predispositions, though these no doubt play their part.

Scientists themselves play an important part in forming our understanding of things, and thereby influence action on many levels. They not only observe but contribute to the construction of reality, on the basis of their own assumptions as well as empirical data. Their knowledge is partial and the information they have is interpreted in the light of existing world views. As knowledge grows, interpretations change, eventually affecting the assumptions underlying them.

There has been much controversy among academics – biologists, anthropologists, historians, political scientists and those who study international relations – about the human predisposition to war. They remain divided, but the pendulum has swung away from the likes of Freud and Lorenz, who see us trapped in the

where?

destructive aspects of our animal nature, and towards the view that human beings are complex and multifaceted, and have the capacity to develop alternate models of philosophy and behaviour. The most widely accepted view now is that the institution of war is mediated and carried through culture.[15]

THE ROLE OF CULTURE

Just as our lives are affected by structures, we know that we (like others) are influenced by the patterns of thought, expression and behaviour within which we live. These sets of patterns can be described as 'cultures'. Although many societies now include people from a variety of cultural backgrounds, and in any case no culture is monolithic but subject to myriad variations and contradictions, culture remains a complex but important factor to be reckoned with. The structures of state and army are culturally reflected in flags and anthems.

According to Johan Galtung,[16] cultures, structures and actions form a mutually influential triangle. Just as structures (systems and embedded relationships) – political, economic, military and social – have an enormous impact on people's lives, they also play a big part in forming or changing cultures. And cultures, which help to govern the way we think and act, also influence the formation of structures. In particular, the violent aspects of a culture – 'cultural violence' – 'makes direct and structural violence look, even feel, right – or at least not wrong'.[17] So it is that we accept as normal the dominatory models of power discussed above. And so it is that physical violence is ingrained in our cultures.

To illustrate Galtung's idea (which I find entirely convincing), I will take the example of domestic violence: the laws of a country may give a woman inferior status, depriving her of property rights and allowing her husband to 'chastise' her in certain circumstances (cultural violence). This encourages him to abuse her (direct violence) and makes it hard for her to escape from his power. The culture which makes this state of affairs seem acceptable is reinforced by the behaviour of the couple, as well as its embodiment in the laws of the land.

Disrespect for children and their human rights in many countries results in their being kidnapped to serve as child soldiers, and for the poor and marginalised, whether adults or children, war can become the only apparent means of survival. The arms trade, although regarded by many as immoral, is sanctioned by law and justified in terms of profit and employment. Used as a route to wealth and power by those involved in it, it fuels wars all around the world and contributes to their motivation. In all these cases, direct violence is perpetuated by social factors and norms.

In 'modern' society, acceptance of war, and fascination with its technology, forms part of a wider picture of 'cultural violence'. Think of the plethora of violent films, books and toys; the gun culture which is endemic in the US and beginning to make its way into the mores of the young in the UK; the rise of the 'Humvee' – a military-style vehicle – as the car of choice in the US; the fact that a 'trademark lawyer' in the US wanted to patent the words 'Shock and Awe' as a brand name; the embeddedness of violence in our language to a degree that military metaphors are so commonplace that they are no longer taken as such. (I will not give up my doubtless irritating objection to the phrase 'target groups'. Though no one thinks of this phrase as having anything to do with militarism, the very attitude it signifies turns those designated into instruments of someone else's objectives.)

Behind these modern forms of cultural violence and coexisting with them lie the rites and symbols that celebrate violent masculinity as the archetype of strength and courage. Consider the association between the notion of honour and the notion of fighting. Think of spears as symbols of power; of the status attached to military uniforms and the love of military parades; of all the flags, statues and other symbols of militaristic nationalism.

The age-long culture of violence is not only expressed in belief systems and cultures, but subverts them when they point elsewhere. Jesus Christ preached love, humility and the power of powerlessness; yet wars have been fought, soldiers blessed and ships 'christened' in his name.[18] Though the Prophet Mohammed taught tolerance and non-aggression, the *jihad* of spiritual struggle, like St Paul's metaphor for moral battle – 'fighting the good fight' – has often been displaced by outward acts of physical warfare. Buddhism, whose essence is nonviolence, non-separation or oneness, has been used as a platform for nationalism.

GENDER AND VIOLENCE

The 'us–them' framework that is integral to the culture of domination finds its widest and perhaps its deepest expression in the division between women and men. The example which I took to illustrate the workings of the violence 'triangle' was one of domestic violence, in this case the violence of a husband against his wife. This is all too common a phenomenon, globally, amounting to an endemic, invisible war. In some societies mainstream, 'official' culture has shifted away from sanctioning it, but the underlying culture persists and the violence and injustice continue. In other societies this state of affairs is still accepted as 'normal'. Women are regarded as second-class citizens, or even as less than human. A woman's life or a woman's word are not equal to a man's. Different moral standards are applied to them: more is expected of them and less can be expected by them. They are told by men what they can and cannot do. They may be beaten when they 'give cause' for annoyance, treated as 'chattels' or possessions. Their function in life is to do men's bidding and serve their needs. They have no rights even in relation to the children they bear and nurture.

In the UK, the cultural climate and laws have changed, though violence against women and children, often with an explicitly sexual component, remains all too common. In the past, however, it was perfectly 'respectable' for men to dominate or control women and to use physical violence against them. The Church issued guidance as to the implements that could be used for assault, specifying the thickness of the stick and so on. It is still possible, in England, to choose a marriage service in which a woman submits herself to her husband, promising to obey him, and in many other parts of the world such a relationship of domination and submission would be taken for granted.

Such relationships are founded on a model of power which assumes that 'might', or the physical capacity to bully others, gives the right to do so. (Children also suffer from this immoral assumption – sometimes at the hands of women.)

Through their domination over women, men have traditionally 'proved' their 'manliness'. It is an important element in prevailing models of masculinity that men should be dominant. A man who is not in command of his wife is seen as a figure of fun, comical because he is not a 'real man'. From a position of control he may properly behave 'gallantly', but that is a matter of *noblesse oblige* – the choice of the powerful to act with magnanimity.

It is not a linguistic accident that 'man' is the equivalent of 'human being' in the world's dominant language. (In fact that equivalence is fictitious. Just see the difference in the mind's eye between 'men' and 'people'. Or try substituting 'women' for 'men' and imagine a language in which 'women' was the received equivalent of 'human beings'.)

With a few notable exceptions – quickly named because they are so few – women have been invisible in public life. (That state of affairs is changing, but very slowly and in some countries and cultures more than in others.) Go and buy any newspaper and look at the photographs in it: politics, national and international, business, sport. There may be one or two women, but not many (in my 'culture', perhaps only the one who has most of her clothes off, for men to enjoy). It is often argued that women and men need not have the same roles to be regarded by each other as equal or to experience equality. (That must depend on who decides the roles.) However, it is not simply a matter of who does what, but of whose activities and roles are valued – for instance, what is found to be sufficiently important to be in a newspaper. And that is not, apparently, the things that women do.

The invisibility of women has a historic perspective. The dominant history, which has shaped our perceptions of humanity, has been the story of the public actions of dominant members of the dominant sex – with war as the most noteworthy and 'glorious' form of public action.

In 'modern' societies, in civilian life, aggressive behaviour in adult men is less acceptable than it used to be. Still, behaviour that is seen as aggressive in women is found acceptable and described as, for instance, 'forceful' in men. These different standards are more striking when applied to children. People laugh when little boys fight and say that 'boys will be boys', recreating on a daily basis the notion that to be properly male is to be aggressive. Fighting is seen as an aberration in little girls. They, by contrast, are expected to be gentle and caring. (Mothers often play a lamentable part in this inconsistency, and so do school teachers.)[19]

In most modern societies the aggressive and antisocial behaviour of (some) young men creates problems. (In the West, similar behaviour among young women is on the rise, though still overshadowed by male aggression.) It is inescapable that when we think of violence (in general) we think – first and foremost – of men, or of men-in-the-making. When we think of wars, and images of war, the same is true.

Young men are prepared by society for war. Here I cannot resist borrowing a quotation from Jonathan Glover,[20] who cites Tim Lynch, a veteran of Britain's war against Argentina in the Falklands. Lynch describes how the moral norms of daily life are broken down by drawing on a deep-seated notion of what constitutes masculinity:

> Take a young man, desperate to establish an identity in the adult world, make him believe military prowess is the epitome of masculinity, teach him to accept absolutely the authority of those in command, give him an exaggerated sense of self-worth by making him part of an elite, teach him to value aggression and dehumanize those who are not part of his group and give him permission to use any level of violence without the moral restraints which govern him elsewhere.

In the service of this construction of masculinity as aggressive, women at times goad men to greater violence – for instance, distributing white feathers to men not enlisting in World War I or identifying potential victims for slaughter in the Hutu genocide against Tutsis in Rwanda. Through such displays of supportive aggression they may be playing out a 'non-feminine' aspect of their own personality, but they are also making their own gender roles subservient to those of their men.

In fact, as recent discussion of war trauma confirms, to commit acts of extreme violence does not come naturally to most people. Soldiers have to be trained and 'psyched up' for it, because it goes against the grain, and are liable to be profoundly disturbed after it. Post-traumatic stress among soldiers has acquired the status of a recognised syndrome. It is probably true for most of us that the things we ask them to risk and to do in our name are not things we would dream of doing ourselves. (In the UK at least recruitment to a volunteer army has become more difficult – despite the existence of a large pool of marginalised young people who have in the past seen military service as their only hope of obtaining regular employment and acquiring qualifications. A military spokesman recently put this down to the need to 'compete' with other potential employers, apparently not considering the nature of the work as inherently unattractive and out of step with civil norms.)[21]

While our image of war is an image of men, when we think of the victims of war, the picture changes: 'women and children' come into view. This is their role. (Older men are invisible, fitting neither the aggressor nor the victim category.) While many civilians are killed 'by accident', women are also the objects of particular and deliberate violence. As noted in Chapter 2, the 'use' of sexual violence – above all against women – is an 'act of war': a way in which the perpetrator asserts his dominance and humiliates the person to whom the woman 'belongs'. She is not only humiliated and violated directly, but is used as an instrument of humiliation. And after war domestic violence and wider sexual violence against women and children is particularly high.

The model of male sexuality that this reflects is one of aggression and control and is inextricably linked with the violence of war. Cultural historian Riane Eisler, whose concept of 'domination' I have adopted, points to a profound connection between this model of sexual relationship and the ills that beset us at every level of society, from domestic to international.[22]

NATURE AND NURTURE: CHANGING GENDER ROLES

Here we come back to the question of human nature. Is this model of male–female relationship 'natural' and therefore inevitable? Do men have to be aggressive and women submissive? There is an ongoing debate among feminists, between those who see men and women as 'essentially' different and those who regard the gulf between them as largely created by the 'social construction' of gender.

Wherever the balance lies between nature and nurture, if we move from the world of theory to the world of experience, we can see that culture plays a major part. Culture, though it can be self-perpetuating, is also changeable: witness the major changes that many of us have seen in our own lifetimes. There have also been different models in the past. In *The Chalice and The Blade*, Eisler argues that there have been thriving societies characterised by co-operative, egalitarian relationships. Those societies were, notably, characterised by equality in male–female relationships.[23]

It is important to note that in Eisler's examples gender equality is one essential and formative aspect of a culture founded on co-operation rather than domination. One lamentable element in the liberation process from which women in 'modern' societies have, by and large, benefited has been that women have sometimes been drawn into the culture of aggression which is part of the dominatory model of human relationships.

I do not see the involvement of women in militarism (whether as soldiers in the state army, as guerrilla fighters or as suicide bombers), or the increase in antisocial behaviour among young women and girls, as cultural progress. It is tilting the culture further in the wrong direction. We will all be the losers if this culture of domination – of the control of the weak by the strong and the few by the many – is confirmed rather than undermined by the 'liberation' of women. That liberation will be no liberation at all, but a further step towards the abyss.

Ironically, changes in women's roles are often precipitated by war, since, in the absence of the men who are fighting, women take on the roles that in peacetime are occupied by their husbands. They become the heads of households and the only breadwinners, often having to move away from their homes to escape the violence that threatens to engulf them.

When war is over, there is a tendency for them to be expected to return to their former status as subservient partners. Nonetheless, they have proved that the functions they fulfilled while the men were away are well within their capabilities and that it is not nature but culture that has assigned to them their 'normal' role.

These pattern shifts, whether temporary or permanent, illustrate the capacity of human beings to adopt new models of relationship and behaviour. I know that I am capable of a high degree of aggression. I am equally capable of care and kindness. In the expression or suppression of either capacity, I exercise choice and am influenced by many things, which collectively can be described as culture. While the family culture in which I was raised played a strong role in my development, the cultural influences of the wider society in which I live have played a major part, even when I have reacted against them. And those influences have changed during my lifetime. We have the power, and also the responsibility, to change our cultures for the better. Given their existing primary role in raising children, women have a particular role in this.

To draw out and reward the brutal side of any human being and to discourage their gentler, more creative and caring characteristics is to disrespect and diminish their humanity and to stifle their moral resources. I believe that men's humanity is violated as much as women's by culturally dominant approaches to masculinity and power. Within the male world there is huge pressure to conform and to compete. For those whose nature does not equip them to do this successfully, this means constant pressure, humiliation and 'failure'.

What we all need is the possibility to be ourselves to the fullest of our ability. This is not a matter of selfishness or the denial of social responsibilities, which does not bring fulfilment. It means bringing the best of ourselves to the lives of our communities, whatever form those communities take.

BROADER POSSIBILITIES OF CULTURAL CHANGE

The culture and structures of violence, which result in the degradation of so many and which fuel and 'justify' war, are in desperate need of changing. I believe that cultural change is fundamental if we are to address the structures that maintain inequality and to outlaw war as an expression of identity and a means of exercising power.

Cultures, like structures, are not fixed things, but complex collectivities of attitudes, behaviours and processes. They change as people and their circumstances change. We may react against our own culture (though the price may be high) or we may choose, more or less consciously, to fit in with it. Either way it affects us. If we choose to live by a different set of patterns or norms and if there are enough others like us, our collective behaviours and attitudes may be described as a 'counter-culture'.

Even without such radical departures, all cultures are open to change. Sometimes change happens very fast; at others it is almost imperceptibly slow. Either way, it happens because the people who live within that culture not only are formed by it but also form it. Just as inherited characteristics affect the course of our lives but do not determine it, so culture influences us but does not, of itself, decide our actions and opinions. In the way they think, talk and behave, people maintain or change the cultures and structures within which they live, whether they benefit from them or suffer under them.

Let us return to the example of the woman who was subjected to domestic violence. If she chose to respond differently, for instance, to run away to a women's shelter and find some form of gainful employment, or if someone else intervened successfully on her behalf, or the law changed to make the husband's action illegal or to give his wife some financial power in their relationship, or the cultural norms of their society no longer sanctioned his behaviour to her, any one of these things – behavioural, structural or cultural – would influence the other two and his stranglehold on her would be broken. He might also, eventually, be changed.

Things and people do change – are changed – for good and ill. We have a rather short view of history: one in which wars and conquest have played a seemingly constant role. But there are students of human affairs who paint another, more complex (and encouraging) picture. Historians like John Keegan and Riane Eisler, and sociologists like Elise Boulding, have shown that not all societies have used war as a means of conducting human relationships. And anthropologists, like Brian Ferguson (whose work has already been cited in Chapter 2) and Raymond Kelly,[24] have demonstrated that the institution of war appeared relatively late in human evolution. Even in today's frightening global situation, so widely influenced by violent structures and cultures, wars are avoided or ended, and injustices addressed, by co-operative or nonviolent means.[25] (More of this in Chapter 5.)

This should not surprise us, since in Western civil life, as in many other cultures, many daily transactions, organisations and activities are founded on co-operation and respect. Society is not a monolith but a complex, changing mesh of relationships, systems and dynamics. While there may be powerful tendencies in one direction, there may be many things (people, institutions, practices) going in another – like a tide and its undertow. While the big picture may be one of domination, other things may be happening which are just as 'real', based on values of respect and co-operation rather than competition or exploitation.

These alternative, counter-cultural tendencies and substructures are based on a different model of power from the 'power *over*' model. Power can mean the capacity to do – and create – good, life-enhancing things: power *to*. It can mean the ability to act together with others to achieve shared goals: power *with*. It can be given to us by others so that we can exercise some kind of responsibility for their benefit: power *for*. Co-operation may itself involve hierarchies, but hierarchies of service rather than domination, their authority vested in them by invitation and agreement. These approaches to power are associated with positive human capacities, in particular our capacity for co-operation.

In many countries we have seen our civil arrangements move largely away from ones of explicit domination enforced by violence (even though violent means of enforcement remain in the wings and are sometimes used quite crudely). For instance, in the UK gun ownership is largely outlawed, and in a recent poll of British police officers (despite a rise in violent crime) a large majority said they did not want to carry arms. While we are extremely worried at the gun (and knife) culture that has arisen in some areas, I believe that most British people would feel less rather than more secure if all our police started to carry guns; and I think it is because of these positive cultural shifts that so many people are increasingly uneasy about war. They are torn between their habitual acceptance of it as necessary in some circumstances and a growing awareness that it contradicts the values by which they live, day to day.

Many people are uncomfortable about the enforcement of the divisions between the haves and have-nots and try to 'do their bit' by buying Fair Trade products and giving at least some of their income to 'charity'. They are willing to vote for policies to distribute wealth and care for the environment, even if, personally, they find it hard not to enjoy the privileges that they have inherited. And there is a substantial, if fluctuating, anti-war movement. This may have been, so far, a quite inadequate response to the problems of structural and cultural violence, but it means that their sway is far from total and that there is a basis for change. As Eisler puts it, we are 'cocreators of our social evolution'.[26]

PSYCHOLOGY AND MORAL DEVELOPMENT

At the end of *Humanity*, Jonathan Glover wrote, 'It is too late to stop the technology. It is to the psychology that we should now turn.'[27]

Psychologists have described in various ways the moral development of human beings, from birth to adulthood. It was once argued that boys developed their capacity for moral judgement more rapidly than girls. However, Carol Gilligan, in her book *In a Different Voice*,[28] argued that this was because moral development was being assessed in male terms. Girls, she said, had a different approach to assessing moral issues. While boys' moral sense was focused on justice, girls were more concerned with care. Boys tended to separate things out and choose between them, girls to bring them together and integrate them.

I see these two tendencies, whether 'essential' or culturally based, as complementary. The capacity to differentiate and choose is an important aspect in the exercise of moral responsibility. Indeed, it has been argued that it is essential to thought of any kind.[29] But the capacity to hold different arguments and needs together, to integrate ideas and elements, is also of fundamental importance. And the value and impulse of caring are vital to our wellbeing, both as care givers and care receivers. (According to Eisler there is a well-established, positive connection between caring for others and the health of the carer.)[30]

A more integrative and inclusive approach to judgement and decision-making could help us to modify current oppositional attitudes and systems in public life. In the UK these are exemplified by rowdy debates in Parliament, 'three-line whips' for voting and a 'first past the post' 'winner takes all' voting system. We see them also in the adversarial system in our law courts. A more integrative approach could help us to act more productively and wisely; to escape from the 'us or them' syndrome of separation, of which the crudest manifestation is war.

In Chapter 6 I shall return to the question of identity and belonging. What I want to focus on here is our apparent 'need', from childhood, to divide people into 'goodies and baddies' in a way that supports the us–them dichotomy at the root of dominatory behaviours, and structures and cultures. This tendency is both expressed and reinforced by myths and archetypes (whether religious or not) in which good and evil are personified. Even where this personification is plainly symbolic, I believe it embodies and encourages our inclination to categorise others in simplistic and distorting ways. (I have made myself unpopular by saying this about the current enthusiasm for J. R. R. Tolkien's *Lord of the Rings*.)

In *The Gulag Archipelago*, Aleksandr Solzhenitsyn challenges this dualism:

> If only it were all so simple! If only there were evil people somewhere insidiously committing evil deeds and it were necessary only to separate them from the rest of us and destroy them. But the dividing line between good and evil cuts through the heart of every human being and who is willing to destroy a piece of his own heart?[31]

Perhaps we are afraid of our own capacity for evil and so project it on to others. Perhaps we are so little reconciled to the human condition of frailty and mortality that we console ourselves by blaming others and doing our best to control them, since we cannot control our own life and death. Perhaps in some way, at some stage of our development, such paranoia contributed to the survival of those who suffered from it.

Whatever the explanation for our psychological malfunctions, we can choose to manage and adjust them to serve us better in the present. There is a growing body of thinking on human development, over and above existing theories on the taken-for-granted development of individual human beings as they grow from babies into adults. As we are exposed to new experiences, information and thinking, our own understanding and perspective is enlarged. Recent research suggests that experience and thought can change the very chemistry and organisation of the brain.[32] If we recognise the impact of prevailing cultural constructs and patterns on us, we will want to change them, as we change ourselves.

In the eyes of many secularists (and indeed religious people), religion is responsible for much that is wrong with the world. And indeed religion has been used to justify and support much cruelty and violence.[33] But materialistic ideologies have also left their own trail of human misery. I would argue that, like other cultural influences, religion can be a source of support for both creative and destructive thinking and action. Whatever our belief systems, we need to take responsibility for them and measure them by the most fundamental and universal standards, our own deepest values and conscience.[34]

The writings of the main world religions contain much exhortation to their readers to respect and care for each other and to eschew violence, as well as passages which seem to support domination and cruelty. They reflect the world views of their writers and are interpreted differently by people living in different situations and times; and different individuals select different passages to support their own values. Religions, like their adherents, both help to form culture and are formed by it. They are understood differently by different individuals and used to support or inspire different points of view.

In the name of religion people have tortured, murdered and conquered. They have oppressed women, taught hatred and blown themselves and others to pieces. But equally in the name of religion people have dedicated their lives to the service of others, abolished slavery, taught liberation and campaigned for justice. Religion is a potent cultural force and sometimes a strong motivator. Like other ideologies, it offers a strong framework for thinking and acting. But as a Muslim friend said to me once, inspiration is as important in the interpretation of what is written as it was in the writing.

Eisler argues that we are directed by culture to a preoccupation with sin and pain rather than creativity and pleasure. She points to religious sources of this tendency and also to new thinking, which redeems what is most positive in our religious and other cultural traditions, and fills the woman- and pleasure-shaped gaps in them.[35]

Eisler's theory may offer some explanation for the sad reality that goodness can seem very dull. Some readers may remember examination questions on Milton's *Paradise Lost*: why did Adam seem so dull in comparison to Satan? (Eve is portrayed as something of a simpleton – though her argument for eating the apple has in fact some 'bite'!) Recently I heard the following proverb: 'It is better to live one day as a lion than a hundred years as a sheep.' Although it came from someone else's culture, it reminded me that my recurrent childhood nightmare was of finding myself in heaven, condemned to an eternity of being good, in the company of good people!

We need excitement, it seems, and no doubt there are good evolutionary reasons for that. War is, doubtless, exciting. It brings those involved in it to the very brink of life and death, giving those who wage it the possibility of godlike powers. During the war on Iraq I heard a TV reporter speaking with breathless exhilaration and saying, 'I had to think back to Vietnam to think of anything quite so violent.'[36]

Does modern life present some of us with too little challenge? Does it fail to provide outlets for our urge to act with courage and determination – an urge described as 'aggression', whose Latin root means advancing rather than attacking, suggesting that this is an energy which can be positively channelled. Maybe we do need more challenges of this kind. Perhaps, too, our ultimate powerlessness to control our own fate or defeat mortality makes destruction attractive, since it can give us a power 'fix' and is far easier than creating anything. That is why winning the war is easier than winning the peace. Maybe the myth of war takes its strength from our inability to accept the realities of the human condition, to bear the frustration of limited powers and the fact of vulnerability – just as to burn down a school or shoot some classmates may, to an alienated adolescent, feel better than remaining powerless.

Maybe. But, once again, we must find non-harmful ways of meeting this need. Overcoming that sense of alienation, exclusion and powerlessness would be a start. There is plenty of scope for heroism and risk-taking without war. If we need to take risks, to go to the point where life and death are in the balance, there are some very good channels for doing so – for instance, rescuing other people from the various kinds of calamity that will continue to be part of our human condition even if we can rid ourselves of disasters of our own making.

We must and can discover and develop our own creative powers and find excitement and pleasure in what we can make and share together. We must give our children and young people a sense of their own worth and place in society. We must provide them with the care and support that will demonstrate it to them and create new forms of community where society has become fragmented. We must learn to enhance our own sense of identity and wellbeing by celebrating and enhancing the wellbeing of others. And we can assuage our frustration at our limitations and our fear of mortality by coming to terms with who and what we are in the universe. We can learn to find transcendence in the enduring and universal realities that we experience even in the transience of our own changing world and short lives.

In order for us to live up to the values which we, significantly, name 'humane', and in order for us and our planet to survive, we need to develop other capacities which are equally a part of us: those of empathy, communication and co-operation. We need to use our intellectual abilities in the service of each other, with each other.

Just as people can learn to think and act brutally, so they can learn to think and act with care and respect. They can be brought up to fight and compete, or to play and co-operate. The boundaries between these two approaches will never be sealed or permanent – otherwise they would not be changeable. But we can choose to move away from our emphasis on difference and antagonism and towards a concerted focus on a search for common ground and mutually supportive ways of working.

The systems we have developed (for instance, global capitalism and militarism) are so entrenched that it is hard to see a way out. Our human nature may always subvert our utopian aspirations. But just as in civilian life we manage our 'antisocial' impulses, we can – surely – learn to manage our economic and international relationships more justly and constructively. History records changes of all kinds, and they were brought about – at least in part – by human agency. Politics can evolve in line with changing values and in turn modify or reinvent systems. And since we are all part of the whole, each of us can contribute to change.

'If we are divided, we shall perish.' So said former NATO General Secretary, George Robertson.[37] He was referring to the survival of NATO, but he spoke a greater truth.

4
Peace, War and Ethics

War is always a defeat for humanity.
Pope John Paul II, spring 2003

War ... remains an anomaly in a civilised world.
Committee of the International Red Cross, 1945

Wars must cease to be an admissible institution.
Professor Joseph Rotblat, Nobel Prizewinner, 1996

Reason, as the highest legislative moral power, absolutely condemns war, as a test of rights and sets up peace as an immediate duty.
Immanuel Kant, *Perpetual Peace*

What we do in war – which, after all, lasts a comparatively short time – affects the whole character of peace, which covers a much longer period.
Bishop George Bell in a speech to the House of Lords,
9 February 1944

Ethics may seem like an intellectual abstraction, but we are all, in our own ways, ethicists. In this chapter I want to take apart the moral assumptions that are regularly made about war and relate them to the ethical norms that underpin peace.

ETHICS, SELF AND SOCIETY

It is essential to our humanity that we are moral beings. For most of us it is important to feel that we have behaved well and to be seen by others to have done so. Even when people behave badly and choose not to admit it, they will do their best to justify their actions. The very fact that arguments about what is and is not 'moral' are so common, and often so heated, is evidence of our innate concern with what is right and wrong.

Our sense of what is ethical or moral is closely related to what we value or find important. At present, particularly in Western societies, rapid technological, economic and social change has brought with it a crisis of values, in which many people feel a loss of any sense of moral direction and 'meaning'. Whether the meaning of life is something 'out there' or something we construct for ourselves, it seems to be important to us and, though it cannot be proved, it seems likely that the sharp and sustained rise in suicides is related to a growing sense of 'meaninglessness' – particularly among young people. An ethical framework combined with a strong sense of values is good for our mental health.

Ethical frameworks are essential not only to our psychological wellbeing as individuals, but also to the wellbeing of the societies that we create together and on which we rely for our day-to-day needs and for our security and identity. If we are to live together in relative comfort, we need agreed moral norms, whether expressed as laws or as socially accepted standards of behaviour. Our moral resources make coexistence possible and are the ground of whatever degree of peace we are able to enjoy. The business of ethics, of applying moral principles to human society, is a philosophical one, but it is also necessarily practical. Ethics that cannot work are not ethics at all. By the same token, pragmatism that sets aside ethical considerations is not really pragmatic, since society without an ethical basis would be unworkable.

When we think about the ethics of war and peace we are thinking beyond local communities to global society. Is there enough of a human foundation for agreement on moral fundamentals? I believe there is. Although our sense of morality is closely related to the cultures and structures of the particular societies in which we live, after a lifetime of working across cultural boundaries I am convinced that there are values and experiences that transcend cultural differences and can provide the basis for peaceful coexistence.

Time, place and circumstances clearly bring with them different challenges, insights and interpretations. What, then, can provide the necessary moral basis for ethics that can work in an ever-shrinking world? Immanuel Kant's answer to this question was unequivocal. He held that human beings have an 'obligation to acknowledge, in a practical way, the dignity of humanity in every other man [meaning person]'.[1] This seems an excellent basis for an ethics of human relationships, implying both unconditional respect and practical care or benevolence. (Indeed it would be an excellent basis for our relationship to all beings.)

ETHICS AND WAR

Those who support war, whether enthusiastically or reluctantly, do so in moral terms. Yet the ethical norms and boundaries that make our everyday life together manageable are incompatible with the actions that together constitute war. In war, where the culture of violence is played out and intensified, the peaceful values of civilian life are flouted in extreme ways, violating the humanity of civilians and soldiers alike. That is why one of the side effects of war is the very high incidence of suicide amongst those directly involved in it, once they return to a society 'at peace'. In the UK, according to Ministry of Defence figures, the number of suicides among veterans of the first Gulf War is almost five times the number of those who lost their lives in the war itself, and one homeless person in four is a former member of the 'armed forces'.

It is precisely because war is an onslaught on all universal and humane values that 'Just War' theories have been formulated to justify it. At the same time, as we have seen, the myth of war's heroism, inevitability and efficacy is so deeply embedded and the culture and structures of domination so strong that this contradiction is deeply buried. The result, I believe, is that Just War theories are given too ready credence. Those who do not altogether reject war are in a comfortable majority and are not often pressed to address the moral contradictions inherent in their position. Those who reject it in principle, by contrast, constantly find themselves with their backs to the wall and are expected to have an answer for every dilemma and all the horrible situations that a war society produces. I believe that war is a phenomenon that should exercise the moral faculties of every one of us, to the point where we force ourselves to find a way out of it.

Until we do so our acceptance of war as 'normal' and 'inevitable' will continue to have an inestimable cost. It is this very acceptance that perpetuates war as an institution and all the misery it brings, both directly and indirectly. The impoverishment that comes in its wake and results from the diversion of resources sucked into the war machine, the inequities that war creates and preserves, cause great misery to those who suffer from them and deep moral unease to the rest of us – if we are not morally dead. And while the daily lives of the poor are grim and precarious, those of the more 'fortunate' are also marred by feelings of insecurity: fear of attack from one source or another, and bleak uncertainty about the future.

To be insecure is part of the human condition, but to feel such a *level* of insecurity in an age where we have greater-than-ever possibilities for meeting human needs is a sign that we are being undermined by our own attitudes and systems: those that pit us against each other rather than enabling us to be co-creators and guarantors of each others' safety and wellbeing. Militarism is the apotheosis of the unethical aspects of our cultures and structures that so threaten our wellbeing: personal, social, financial, ecological and political. It undermines the care and respect which alone can make life secure or fulfilling.

ETHICS AND POWER

As I argued in Chapter 3, war is an expression of power as the ability to control others: power *over*. Power of this kind is based on 'might', rather than 'right'. Such a concept of power is essentially amoral. The philosopher Nietzsche,[2] seen by many as contributing to the moral atmosphere in which Nazism was possible, gloried in naked, violent (masculine) power and saw moral scruples and care (feminine) as weakness and a block to greatness. By contrast, most of us, even if we accept that some people should in certain circumstances have power over others, believe that such power can be abused and in our more idealistic moments would think that its use was valid only in the service of good. We also want to guard against its possible damaging effects. In other words, we subject it to ethical scrutiny and do not see it as desirable in its own right.

Control-power may sometimes need to be exercised for the protection or wellbeing of someone or something. It may be exerted through social pressure, or by moral, organisational or legal authority that has broad recognition and respect.[3] This power, ideally, is based on collective will or consent and is exercised *with* or on behalf of others *for* some good purpose. When a society, on whatever scale, is working well, that controlling power rarely needs to be exercised, since what is done within and on behalf of the collective is generally supported. When for whatever reason consent is withdrawn, the first line of action is to find out why and try to restore it. If as a temporary expedient or in exceptional circumstances enforcement is needed (power *over*) for the general good, the principle for such enforcement is to restrict it to what is absolutely necessary and to avoid infringing the human rights of the person or group to whom it is applied. The goal will be the eventual restoration of the relationship of that individual or group to the rest of society. When a society is working well, enforcement is carried out in such a way as to honour and uphold, rather than infringe, the legal and social norms that are being defended. It is able to prevail *and* comply with moral norms because it has overwhelming support.

When power *over* is used in relation to another, non-consenting society, the whole dynamic changes. 'Enforcement' becomes violence on a massive scale against an entire society (whatever the 'spin' to the contrary). War is a wholesale infringement of civil norms, sweeping aside due processes of justice and human rights. Its peacetime equivalent would be assassinations and mass executions without trial. Our weapons of mass destruction could kill far more people than Hitler's gas chambers and are ready for use. We have lived with this shocking reality for so long that our ethical sensibilities have been deadened. War and its machinery erode and corrupt our capacity to distinguish between right and wrong. It sits like an ugly colossus in the midst of our apparently civilised society and serves to perpetuate the very uncivilised global injustices that deny to so many fellow human beings the barest minimum of what is needed to sustain humanity.

THE LOGIC (AND ILLOGIC) OF WAR

Outside the context of consent, the power to impose one's will on another group comes purely from violence – and 'superior' violence at that. The logic of war makes the application of peacetime values impossible. Decisions have to be made first and foremost on the basis of what will give military advantage – gaining control of a territory, establishing new bases, destroying or capturing weapons, 'taking out' potential opposition.

In war it is bad to be weak. Iraqi friends tell me that it was felt as a matter of shame that Iraqi troops were not able to put up a 'decent fight' against the invaders. And at the time of the Iraq war Russian nationalists were campaigning to have Ivan the Terrible beatified, his 'virtue' being that he was a strong leader and brought power and honour to Russia. Both Saddam Hussein and Ivan the Terrible were tyrants, but one was outgunned, and therefore without honour. (And since might is right, it is always the losers who are held accountable for war atrocities, not the winners.) In a 'suicide bombing', to kill large numbers of people is to succeed. Logic based on success in things that contravene everyday morality is bound to undermine ethical norms. Within the logic of war, human beings, who should be the focus of ethical concern, are lost in the big picture of military strategy.

War obliterates moral boundaries[4] and gives the lie to the moral constraints that we try to apply to it. Since, as we have seen, its logic demands that losses to one's own side should be limited, that requirement all too often means that civilians are sacrificed as 'collateral damage'. It means that bombs and cluster bombs are used because they are militarily effective, though devastating to civilians, and that warheads are strengthened with radioactive uranium to ensure that they penetrate their targets, in spite of the terrible birth deformities and cancers to which their use will give rise. It means that it is all too likely that humanitarian considerations will be secondary (to say the least) in the interrogation of prisoners, since they are such an important source of information.

It is ironic that war is so strongly linked to the notion of honour, when in the reality of war the rudiments of 'fair play' make no sense. Iraq was ruined by sanctions and its most potent weapons were destroyed before war was launched against it. As Arundhati Roy so pungently put it, 'Operation Iraqi Freedom' was 'more like "Operation Let's Run a Race, but First Let Me Break Your Knees"'.[5] And when 100 Iraqi soldiers were holding their own in a gunfight with 500 US troops at Um Qasr, the US soldiers simply bombed them. Such actions go against the sense of justice that constitutes a moral resource in everyday life.

Likewise truthfulness, a value prized in most societies, is a liability in war. Communication becomes a weapon to be used for strategic advantage. 'Spin' and presentation take the place of open reporting. Deception and subterfuge are necessary, both politically and militarily.

In the wealthy West, the contrast between the wholesale slaughter of war and the extraordinary lengths to which we go to preserve life in peacetime (and even sometimes in war itself) is so great as to be difficult to grasp. We find impairment and mortality so unacceptable that we will go to almost any lengths to overcome them. Advances in surgical and medical techniques have made all kinds of rescue operations, including human transplants, possible. Doctors will spend years preparing conjoined twins for separation and more years, if they succeed, supporting their recovery. New possibilities in plastic surgery have brought us to the point where whole faces can be reconstructed or even replaced. And yet in a moment we are prepared to cause injuries on a scale and of a nature too horrible to contemplate.

The gulf between the logic of war and the logic of everyday decency and justice gives rise to moral confusion and contradiction. While the enemy's weakness is a matter for scorn, and success in killing them is cause for celebration, if they manage to kill any of 'our' troops it is a matter for resentment, not respect. *We* fight for humanity and honour, but *they* fight for fanatical nationalism. *We* wear camouflage colours to hide ourselves but *their* lack of 'proper' uniforms, which makes it hard for us to spot them, is cheating. *They* should stick to 'honest and open combat' in which they can be easily slaughtered by our massively 'superior' firepower. In fact, they should not fight back at all, because by doing so they block the delivery of humanitarian aid. They should have the good sense to surrender, run away or come over to our side (though 'desertion' on our side would be unforgivable).

Despite their second-class 'peacetime' status and the ugly fact of their subjection to sexual violence, in war 'women-and-children' are, paradoxically, regarded as more human than men, worthy of special protection. I confess to feeling that this is just as well, but I cannot see any defence for it on ethical grounds, if ethics is based on common humanity. The vulnerability that in 'their' soldiers is derided, in their 'women-and-children' becomes a matter of moral status. But then why do we ask some of our fellow citizens to give up their humanity and be combatants on our behalf? And how is it that we give a higher value to the lives and safety of our own troops than to those of 'enemy' civilians?

Any ethical system based on the unconditional recognition of humanity is stood on its head in war. People are to be killed if they pose a threat to the success of your side, or to you if you are a soldier. Practically speaking, it is not possible to engage in a war, let alone win it, without suspending the human status of enemy soldiers and regarding them as fair targets for killing. That is how war works. But that is not an ethical reason for killing them. Nor is the fact that they are fighting for someone designated 'The Enemy'.

Not only is it outside our ethical norms to kill people deliberately – even if they are committing crimes – but they may have reasons for fighting which are ones which should, within the logic of war, be taken into account. They may be acting under duress, or from a sense of national honour, or to protect their homeland and fellow citizens, or because they think they should obey orders, or do what they are paid to do – just like our soldiers.

Our attitude to our own 'service' men and women is itself confused. Even though we set great store by their physical safety, we deny their moral and emotional humanity by nature of the actions they are required to take on our behalf – actions whose traumatising effects are at last beginning to be recognised.

To join the army is to be deprived of moral choice. A soldier cannot opt out of a particular war because he or she sees it as wrong, or disobey orders once under engagement. Two British soldiers were sent home from the Gulf for refusing to obey orders, in obedience, they said, to their conscience. The military spokesperson interviewed by the BBC commented that at a time of war they had no right to question the instructions of their commanding officer. Except, presumably, if 'war crimes' were in question, as against all the other brutal and lethal acts that they are ordered to carry out. Then obedience would become a crime in itself. (But as I have said, victors are not often held to account. If they are, it is the 'little men' who take the rap.)

A system for the management of international relations that requires those involved to suppress or deny their own conscience, to overcome their humane impulses and to transgress the ethical norms of civil society cannot, I would argue, be considered an ethical institution, contributing to the long-term good of humanity.

WAR AS JUSTICE

The punishment rhetoric of the War on Terror – 'we must go after them and bring them to justice' – is in line with one of war's age-old justifications. It is the blood feud writ large and carries the same connotations of honour and retribution. These are ethical concepts, but are they ones that we should accept? Are they in line with the notion of what is humane – of respect and care for human beings? And do they have anything to do with fair play?

In the case of America's wars on Afghanistan and Iraq, the notion of 'scapegoats' seems to fit better than the concept of justice. A crime had been committed against the US and someone had to be punished – as if a god had to be appeased and suitable victims found. Afghanistan may have harboured terrorists, but those who caused so many deaths on 11 September prepared and carried out their attacks from within the US and were connected to groups operating in European countries. Similarly, in the case of Iraq, no convincing or adequate connection with Al Qaeda, let alone with those particular atrocities, had been established.

In any case, is ad hoc vengeance, without 'due process', part of the ethics we want to espouse? And is it justice to include people who have played no part in an alleged crime in a brutal form of collective punishment? As I heard someone remark recently, 'You don't bomb Sicily to get rid of the Mafia!' Is the bombing of towns and villages, the destruction of land and infrastructure, the devastation of a heritage, an appropriate form of punishment for the actions of governments (especially despots) or of particular groups acting independently of them? Was the West justified in targeting the USSR with genocidal nuclear weapons, precisely because its regime was repressive? To exterminate people because they are oppressed seems particularly perverse. Indiscriminate acts of retribution by 'terrorists' are morally unacceptable for precisely the same reasons.

War is, by its very nature, general in its impact – that is, it does not confine itself to the killing of particular individuals. It also inflicts punishments that no society would consider ethical and no legal system would sanction. Even countries that still carry out executions would not do so in such inhumane ways – and many have moved away from the legalisation of killing. If the execution of individuals, after a fair trial, is deemed by the governments of so many countries to be unethical, how is it that wide-scale, general killings, barbarously executed, without any trial of those killed, should be considered morally acceptable?

It was bizarre that the unearthing of mass graves of people murdered under Saddam Hussein's tyranny was seen as justification for what was done to Iraq by the US and UK. He brutally killed those who rose up against him and often, apparently, anyone connected with them. That is judged, quite rightly, to be morally outrageous. But if all those blown apart by 'our' bombs were heaped into mass graves and dragged out again, what would be the difference? Through the brutality of war, the moral ground was levelled. Ethically speaking, war is a great equaliser.

JUST WAR THEORIES

The majority of good and sincere people nonetheless support war as an institution. They do so because they believe that in some circumstances the consequences of not going to war would be worse than those associated with war itself. Since the time of St Augustine[6] and probably long before, people have struggled to apply ethical standards to the conduct of war, positing 'just' criteria for engagement and developing rules to regulate the treatment of civilians and prisoners.[7] Since the advent of modern, technological warfare, the concepts of 'Just War' have been codified in the various international Geneva and Hague conventions.

Although much 'Just War' doctrine has Christian roots (though nothing to do with Jesus's precepts), other faiths have their own teaching about war. The Koran sets out rules of war for Muslims and warns against the false god of nationalism. The word *jihad* is often used to mean 'holy war', though its deeper and more general meaning is 'struggle' – first and foremost of a spiritual nature.

The criteria that have been developed for a Just War include the following elements:

- Legitimate authority.
- Just cause (such as defence against unprovoked invasion, or the unseating of tyrants).
- Exhaustion of all other options.

- Proportionality – the likelihood that the war will be successful and that the good achieved will be greater than the cost (morally speaking), and the use of the least destructive means necessary to achieve the war's goal.
- Discrimination between combatants and civilians, with a prohibition against the deliberate killing of the latter.

The notion of legitimate authority seems to have little strength on its own, begging the questions of justice and truth which would make authority legitimate. In recent years the United Nations has been regularly proposed and dismissed as the necessary and appropriate authority for war. Those who claim just cause for a war will argue, one way or another, that they have just authority. The logic of domination of which war is a part goes against the UN's ever being accorded the authority to overrule national self-interest. And those who wish to launch a civil war or to overthrow existing national authorities will deny the legitimacy of those they oppose and claim moral authority for what they do.

The idea of just causes is fundamental to Just War theory and is what makes most good people accept war as necessary. Although I have suggested that most wars are fought for very bad reasons, I would readily agree that there are situations in which it would seem not only desirable but urgent that certain rulers, groups or armies should be prevented from doing certain things. The traditional 'just causes' were those of self-defence by a state against invasion or aggression. The list has gradually been extended to include wars against tyrants or governments that are oppressing their own people, carrying out genocide, or attacking or invading other countries. It has also been argued that it could be justifiable to join a war already under way, to make sure the 'right' side wins.[8]

While I agree that the concept of a 'just cause' for action is valid, I do not believe in the ethical validity of war as a means of achieving such a cause. That is, firstly, because civilians cannot in practice be protected – nor can their environment – though greater or lesser efforts can be made in this direction. Secondly, because 'discrimination' on any grounds (in this case in favour of civilians) is contrary to the nature of human rights, whose ethical foundation is their unconditionality. The wholesale slaughter of soldiers contravenes the essence of human rights. I shall discuss these issues under 'Means and Ends' later.

I argued in Chapters 1 and 2 that, while it is often claimed or implied that all other options have been exhausted so that war has become inevitable, more often than not little serious effort has been made to try other means. Little is done, seriously and on a scale comparable to the scale of militarism, to develop such alternatives.

The nature of the success that needs to be the likely outcome of a war, in terms of its 'just causes' (not simply the military victory which would be necessary to them), is contrary to the nature of war, as I argued in Chapters 2 and 3. War is not the right tool for preventing killing and the like since it consists of those things, nor for building democracy since it is a totalitarian mechanism, nor for developing good relationships for the same reason. More humane and, in the long term, more effective means for achieving humane and just ends are discussed in Chapter 5.

I respect the attempts that have been made to limit the horrors of war and to prevent it from escaping altogether from the moral net. I believe that people more honourable and brave than I am have fought in wars and supported them. I agree that wars may be waged for more or less good reasons, and with more or less cruelty, and that trying to make moral choices in war is better than not doing so. Still, I want to argue that the logic of war makes such rules unsustainable and that Just War theories are ethically unsound. While they may at certain points have done some good within wars, they have the great disadvantage of making war seem more acceptable, so diverting us from confronting its enormity.[9]

THE PROTECTION OF CIVILIANS – SLIDING BOUNDARIES

As I have already suggested, within the *logic* of war, the prohibition against killing civilians is unsustainable. If 'humanity' is all-embracing, the only justification I can think of for singling out civilians for humane treatment is that it is not *necessary* to kill them (since they pose no threat). But often the logic of military advantage decrees that it *is* necessary.

Secondly, I do not believe it is within the *nature* of war for civilians not to be killed, both deliberately and accidentally. It is not realistic to suppose that when soldiers are 'psyched up' for war and in a state of hyper-aggression or fear they will obey this rule in all circumstances, though one might agree that they ought to. Actions will be taken in 'the heat of battle', mistakes will be made and distinctions will become blurred. (The US seemed happy to announce that 200 Ba'ath Party members had been killed as they met in Baghdad. It was not claimed that they were military personnel.) While a war is in progress, those responsible for it are keen to assert the propriety of their side's conduct. But the reports that begin to trickle in afterwards reveal how far from ideal the reality has been (and in the context of war the very word 'ideal' seems misplaced).

The mental blurring of distinctions between combatants and civilians seems to be part of the emotional dynamic of war, whatever the weapons. But where bombs and missiles are in use, the very idea of not killing civilians seems in practice to become more and more inapplicable. In modern warfare far more civilians are killed than soldiers. At the beginning of the twentieth century civilian deaths constituted 20 per cent of the total deaths; by the beginning of this century, it was 80 per cent.[10]

We try to get round this reality by calling the killing of civilians, by impersonal means and as a side effect, 'collateral damage'. We say we didn't mean the civilians to die – that wasn't the point of our action. Our intention was to 'take out' some military target with our bombs and the civilians were killed by accident – even though we knew they would be. (This is called the 'dual effect' theory.)[11]

By recourse to this argument, the Israeli government is able to argue that blowing up houses and all their occupants is justified. They say that the destruction of homes and the killing of people who have nothing to do with acts of violence against Israel was not the purpose of the exercise, which was to eliminate a 'terrorist'. ('Assassinate' would be the proper word here, but it is not used, since – curiously – political assassination is not allowed, although what would normally be seen as extrajudicial killing is a regular feature of war.) The 'suicide bomber', on the other hand, who has no particular target or military aim, may not kill more people than a pilot who drops a bomb on an urban target but is seen as a criminal because he or she cannot claim 'dual effect'.

I have no desire to defend the deliberate murder of civilians. But surely the theory of 'dual effect' is fundamentally flawed – whether used by governments or by 'freedom fighters' who kill civilians (for instance, blowing up soldiers in a place where civilians will be present). If I do something, knowing full well what the consequences will be, then I should expect to be held accountable for those consequences. Discounting the killing of civilians in view of a military or political purpose, or even weighing them against it and finding them an insufficient consideration, seems morally equivalent to killing civilians for such a purpose, which is what suicide bombers would claim to do.

Those who kill civilians without having a military target may have the military purpose of using violence to intimidate and demoralise a population in order to 'terrorise' their opponents into making concessions. This seems remarkably similar to the logic implicit in the bombing of Baghdad. Shock and Awe sounds remarkably similar to Terror and Intimidation, and thousands of civilians were inevitably killed (indeed in many cases civilian targets were chosen). The bombs dropped on Hiroshima and Nagasaki were justified because, it was argued, they would bring the Emperor of Japan to the point of capitulation (which he had probably reached already) and speed up the ending of World War II. Hamas, Islamic Jihad and the Al Aqsa Brigade have justified their bomb attacks on civilians by claiming that they are bound to counter tyranny against the Palestinian people and pointing to the narrowness of their military options. Just War theory would permit none of these atrocities, but the logic of war has overwhelmed it.

Civilians are also killed as a warning to other civilians that they should not support the enemy. This is often so in the case of 'insurgency' or 'liberation struggle'. In Peru, thousands of civilians were killed by the *Sendero Luminoso* (Shining Path – a guerrilla organisation) as well as by government forces. And today civilians are constantly being murdered by the FARC and by government and private militias in Colombia. Just War theoreticians have argued against the 'instrumentalisation' of civilians in such ways – using them as a means to an end. But the logic of war seems to provide 'justifications' even for this. In his book, *Just and Unjust Wars*, Michael Walzer argues that, in certain circumstances, where there are no other military options available, the goal of victory may justify the otherwise unacceptable means used to achieve it.[12] If we look at the actual conduct of recent wars, it is hard not to see the moral boundaries of Just War theory as very pliable indeed.

MEANS AND ENDS: CONSEQUENTIALISM

These 'justifications' take us into the wider realm of what ethicists call 'consequentialism'. This is an offshoot of 'utilitarianism', an ethics based on the notion that the fundamental ethical test for anything is whether it contributes to the greatest happiness of the greatest number.[13] (How that can be measured has long been a matter for debate.) The logic of this is that ethical choices may have bad consequences (or at least less good ones) for minorities. The consequentialist argues that actions that are bad in themselves can be justified if their bad effect is outweighed by the desirability of their outcome (the principle of proportionality).

The principle of 'proportionality' is easy to understand, but hard to apply. One can argue about the application of this principle in particular instances – for example, the use of atomic bombs in World War II, the destruction of dams, the bombardment of cities in this or that stage of the war. One can debate how important a political goal would have to be in order to justify the killing of civilians in particular circumstances by 'guerrilla' fighters – and what number of deaths would be seen as proportionate to that goal.

On what basis are these things to be estimated? How many of ours for how many of theirs – civilians for soldiers, soldiers for soldiers, civilians for civilians? One for one? If so and all are equal in value, the whole war principle – us versus them – is undermined. If not, what justification would there be for the standard chosen? How would one weigh the need to gain military advantage against the 'imperative' to protect civilians and how much strategic gain would need to be weighed against how many lives? And what about the 'side effects' of death by starvation or lack of clean water or medical facilities, or the long-term effects of destroying infrastructure and poisoning land?

Whatever the calculations, consequentialism has no logical limit. That is why consequentialists who start off by saying that civilians should never be 'instrumentalised' end up saying that in certain circumstances that principle could be waived. In practice, once bigger and more deadly weapons are available, military logic makes it highly unlikely that they will not be used by those who possess them, as we have seen.

Atom bombs are rightly considered to be particularly horrible and bad, not only because of their capacity to kill huge numbers of people at once, but also because their effects are not limited in time or place and they cause massive environmental contamination. Nonetheless, new 'tactical' nuclear weapons are being developed, for use rather than 'deterrence'. If winning is one of the key principles of a Just War (or indeed any war), this makes some sense, but it makes nonsense of the claim to avoid civilian deaths – just as the use of 'daisy-cutter' bombs in Afghanistan did. The moral law has become an ass. Or rather, I believe, it has been an ass all along.

'Weapons of mass destruction' of whatever kind are indiscriminate by nature. Most of them are owned by the 'big powers', who have justified their original and continuing development of such weapons in the name of 'deterrence' and war prevention. But they do not prevent the wars waged by those same powers against others and, even during the Cold War, proxy wars between the two major power blocs claimed millions of lives. Furthermore, according to its own theory, deterrence depends on the credibility of what is threatened. Preparedness to carry out the threat is the most fundamental element. The moral status of deterrence is therefore equivalent to that of the damage that it promises.

MEASURING WIDER CONSEQUENCES

The viability of consequentialism as an ethical principle presupposes a capacity to weigh consequences fully and reliably. When one is faced with a choice between actions to take and not take, the options *not* chosen will never be tested and their consequences will remain a matter of conjecture. Even if one looks only as far as immediate physical outcomes, the wager involved may be deemed acceptable and indeed necessary. If the action itself would be considered unethical, that inherent badness is the only thing that can be known with any certainty.

It may be argued that it is necessary to carry the moral responsibility of the inevitable inexactitude of calculations and unpredictability. But to think short-sightedly is not responsible and the further in the long term one looks, the less any reasonable level of certainty becomes and the more unfavourable the likelihood. Even if some immediate 'good' is achieved by committing acts that violate fundamental ethical norms, in complex social and political contexts it is impossible to know what will be the wider outcomes of any particular choice, beyond the most immediate.

What have been and will be the consequences of the wars on Afghanistan and Iraq, not just for those countries and their inhabitants, but for relationships within the regions in which they are situated? For relationships between those and other regions? For international relations more generally? For the future of the United Nations? For the ways in which we deal with our capacity to manufacture and use weapons of mass destruction? For the ascendancy of militarism over international law? I would argue that, even within consequentialist logic, insufficient attention has been given to the wider picture. Recent events underline the size and potential impact of this omission.

But even if we were able to complete the consequentialist balance sheet, does the reduction of moral judgements to mathematics honour the essential nature of ethics, or the benevolence and respect that provide their foundation? A major flaw inherent in 'consequentialism' is that in justifying actions that would otherwise be seen as infringing fundamental moral principles, it undermines the very values upon which this justification depends. It demolishes what Kant called 'categorical imperatives', the unconditional moral requirement to respect the dignity of all human beings. In so doing it strikes at the heart of the concept on which the very notion of human rights is based.[14]

The moral impact of extreme forms of consequentialism (and I would argue that war is an extreme form) is incalculable. In Germany, recently, a debate has begun about the unconditional prohibition against torture.[15] This prohibition, fundamental to the notion of human rights, can be questioned along consequentialist lines. I have long thought that it is far easier to justify torture than to justify war. If someone who was known beyond reasonable doubt to be part of a plan to blow up a building with hundreds of people in it were to be captured, and that person refused to give the information that would enable those lives to be saved, would it not make every sense to torture him or her? In such a situation the 'bad' act would be applied only to one individual, whose culpability might be, if not legally proven, at least relatively sure, and its outcome would be predictable with a fair degree of likelihood. The principle of 'proportionality' would be met, at least in terms of the numbers of people affected.

With more careful consideration one can see that 'information' obtained under torture is as likely as not to be fabricated, since the tortured person would very likely say anything to put an end to it. But in any case, what would be the consequences of deciding that it was morally acceptable to use torture in certain circumstances and to legislate accordingly? What would this do to the torturer, to the maintenance of the broader prohibition against torture, and to our general understanding of the most fundamental human rights as being unconditional? Acts of tyranny *are* tyranny.

The idea of torturing someone for lifesaving information might be an appealing one from the short-term or narrow consequentialist perspective, but it is profoundly demeaning. Its wider, long-term consequences are enormous. From a purely utilitarian perspective, one could sanction the killing of all people with chronic illnesses, for instance, arguing that to do so would free up resources for health care for the majority of healthier people. The transgression of our moral norms would be so fundamental that such a step seems unimaginable – but of course Hitler did have a programme for killing people with disabilities. Tyranny sets aside all categorical imperatives, and so does war.

On the basis of the principle of respect for humanity and for life, the prohibition against killing *per se* is a fundamental one (let alone the kind of indiscriminate and large-scale killing of civilians already alluded to). Killing is not some slight and remediable assault, a small act of disrespect, which is transient or can be retrieved, but a massive and final one.

In the UK, the prohibition against killing extends far into civilian law. Even if one's home is invaded by a burglar, shooting the burglar would be justified only if one's life was in immediate danger. Few people are allowed to own guns and one would not be permitted to do so for the purpose of self-defence. With few exceptions the possession of arms would be regarded here as a contravention of the norms of peace. For the police or for members of the public to launch a deadly attack on an entire community would be quite beyond the pale, even if it were argued that the *people* of that community were not being targeted.

War is not only a massive breach of the prohibition against killing that is fundamental to our coexistence: it contravenes our basic notions of justice. It constitutes extrajudicial, collective punishment of a kind that would be considered an outrage in any other circumstance – indeed, in a way that would be considered a cause for war!

The philosopher Isaiah Berlin argued that our ethics must cope with the fact that often different 'goods' or benevolent purposes are in competition with each other – security and civil liberties, for example.[16] But our need to deal with situations where there are different moral pressures and requirements to be managed makes the preservation of some fundamental, non-negotiable values essential. As an anti-corruption policeman said on the radio recently, integrity must be non-negotiable for the police – even when it means losing cases – otherwise the heart of policing has gone. In the same way, respect for life and humanity must be kept at the heart of our ethical systems, or they will cease to have any meaning.

SINS OF OMISSION

It might be argued that while I concentrate on the weaknesses of consequentialism I am ignoring its moral challenges, I am failing to recognise that one may sometimes have a duty to act, and that sins of omission are just as serious as sins of commission. That argument concerns me greatly. It is one that made many hitherto-pacifists join up in World War II. It split the peace movement during the wars in the former Yugoslavia – particularly in Bosnia.[17] It raises agonising questions in relation to Burundi, Rwanda, Sierra Leone and the Congo. Surely there is a moral obligation for military intervention in such cases?

Let us go back to the classical argument presented to pacifists: that if someone vulnerable in their household were under attack it would be their right and duty to overcome the attacker, killing him if necessary. I have always felt that this was a rather macho argument, and an unreal one. Unless I was especially strong – stronger than the assailant – or had a gun (which I am not allowed to do) and was trained in using it, had it lying conveniently close and out of sight, and was naturally adept and quick (and wearing my glasses at the time), the violent option for defence would be a bad bet for me.

I would have much better chances of doing some good, as well as feeling less morally violated, if I used some other strategy, such as surprise, diversion, playing for time, sounding the alarm or finding a way of communicating with the assailant at a human level. For me to spend valuable time and resources preparing to deal violently with such an eventuality might leave me still as a likely loser, incapable of saving those dear to me by violence. I had better rely on my interpersonal skills – as our police do, to negotiate with or win over those who are threatening violence to others.

To prepare myself to be effective through violence would also be inimical to other aspects of my life, displacing useful activities like learning life-saving techniques, or practising my skills for defusing violence, or caring for my family in other ways.

Our police are highly skilled in dealing with those who threaten violence to third parties. They exercise extraordinary patience and seem able to charm the birds out of the trees. They try at all costs to avoid violence because they know that in any shoot-out there is a grave danger that others will be wounded or killed. (When there is no danger to third parties, they are sometimes less restrained.) The techniques that they use are available to all and are based on psychological understanding and the ability to reach out, persuade or divert.

In recent years vigorous efforts have been made to reduce the number of guns in private hands and to counter the culture of violence. Yet the UK's militaristic, might-based behaviour in the world is inimical to that agenda. It absorbs much needed resources and teaches violence by example. By doing so, it makes me and my fellow citizens less, not more, safe from home-grown violence or terrorist attack from abroad, while it degrades our moral standing in the world. It is not surprising that among the large proportion of the world's population which is excluded from the wealth enjoyed by the West, and insulted by its economic and cultural arrogance, some will support reactive terrorism and other crimes.[18] They are part of the same dynamic of violence.

What I want to illustrate and emphasise is that violent options for intervention are based on violent capabilities, and on the wider system and structures of militarism. These, in turn, express and strengthen the culture of violence and domination described in Chapter 3. They leave those with the biggest capacity for violence in the ascendant, whoever they are and whatever their motives, and starve of resources the positive collective endeavours necessary to peace: those that express and support our respect for each other's dignity and enable us to meet each other's needs.

It is true that within the present militarist dispensation there are times and circumstances which seem to call desperately for intervention of some sort – and we are ill-equipped and unpractised for non-military solutions. But as I have argued in Chapter 2, war's power for good in no way measures up to its reputation or its power to undermine and destroy.

ACCEPTING RESPONSIBILITY

I see that I too am some kind of consequentialist – one who looks not only at the immediate effects of militarism but also at its fundamental, long-term consequences. As one who does not support the existence of international military capacities, or their role in the world, I must accept that, if I had my way, military intervention anywhere would be impossible. As things are at the moment, that might mean that in some given circumstance more people died. It might also mean that the kinds of situation in which that would happen were beginning to decrease; that resources were being freed to address the squalor, ignorance and injustice that make them possible; that other forms of more timely, nonviolent intervention were being resourced on a realistic scale.

Meanwhile, I want those who argue for military intervention in such circumstances to recognise that they cannot have occasional, 'necessary' interventions without the whole military machine that makes them possible – a machine that is fuelled by the arms race, the arms industry and the arms trade; that makes some people intervenors and others the objects of intervention, some winners and some losers; that by its very nature gives all the power to the violently strong and seeks to relegate the rest to the role of victim or dependant; that trains people to commit acts which violate their own humanity; that diverts vast wealth from useful, life-affirming purposes and destroys anything that grows or was built, however old or beautiful; that places the weak at an eternal disadvantage and that undermines the values it sets out to uphold. I want them to acknowledge that an institution for killing is no better than an institution for torture.

I want them to recognise, too, that the very situations that seem to cry out for military intervention arise *because* of militarism, past and present, and the wider system of domination of which it is a part, whether it is carried out by states or tribes or guerrilla fighters or secessionists.

I want them to acknowledge that it is not reasonable to expect those who have opposed a whole line of action – and the system which gave rise to it – to have a magic solution to all its negative consequences, while those who initiated it have none.

I want them to admit that militarism does not on the whole have a track record of well-motivated action, clean fighting and good outcomes, but has rather been the scourge of humanity, carrying the seeds of undoing of any humane endeavour and writing a moral blank cheque for future tyranny. I want them to acknowledge that training people to kill and inflict cruel injuries on our behalf is not just or humane. I want them to agree that finding an exit from the whole system is in itself a moral imperative, whose dilemmas we all share. I want them to join in the development of other ways of addressing the problems of violence, right now in the present, as well as in the longer term.

Those who defend Communism, as an idea that is still valid but has never been properly tried, tend to be laughed at. Militarism is not treated with such acerbity. I think it should be. I think we should decide that it has had enough chances and is incapable of reform; that it is time to look for other ways of standing up for good and defending each other.

When we think of war, it is all too easy to think of a generality, an abstraction. But even the most general categories of human endeavour (or anything else) are made up of particular acts and the beings affected by them. Though generalisations may be necessary to our thinking, if we miss those particularities we miss the true nature of the whole. When we speak of 'civilian casualties' (let alone 'collateral damage') we do not follow the sequence – from the command, to the deed, to its multiple effects. We do not see those people, one by one. We do not look into their lives or imagine the impact of their deaths. We need to see humanity not just as 'crowds in movement',[19] but as the individual persons of whom those crowds are composed.

'Wars will cease when men refuse to fight.' So goes the old pacifist adage. Nowadays most of us who live in the West will never be called upon to fight. All that is needed is our assent. All of us, soldiers and civilians, carry our share of responsibility for what is done by the social and political unit within which we live. We have a moral obligation to exercise whatever power we have for what we believe to be right.

The institution of war is by nature contrary to the moral norms necessary to human society. It is integral to a wider system of domination and exclusion. It constitutes a disaster for humanity and an insult to the majority of its members, who live in want, and an unsustainable assault on the ecology of our planet. Its very nature and internal logic make it incapable of reform. Ethics that sanction war are failing to provide a framework for human wellbeing or to protect the future of the earth. If good ethics are useful ethics, 'Just War' ethics have failed the test. They need to give way to the ethics that uphold the values of peace.

STRENGTHENING PEACE ETHICS

In the words of Brazil's President, Luiz Inacio Lula da Silva, 'Multilateralism represents, on the level of international relations, an advance comparable to democracy in national terms.' Multilateralism means looking for co-operative solutions to international problems: solutions based on the recognition of interdependence and on consent. It also means inclusiveness. Lula da Silva's speech was focused on the desperate plight of those excluded from the benefits enjoyed by a wealthy and powerful global minority and the growing insecurity which was likely to result (for the rich; the poor are already insecure). One of the great attractions of democracy is that the stronger it is, the greater the security enjoyed by its participants.

Peace, as a state where respect prevails, implies meeting the needs of all those within its compass for security and dignity, participation and identity.[20] Peace requires the inclusion of all in the collective exercise of power for the common good. It provides for the wellbeing of the collective not by ignoring the dignity of individuals but by honouring it. It calls us to social and political responsibility, which implies both compliance with agreed and necessary norms and the challenging (and if necessary the contravention of) any that undermine the values of peace.

At the same time, by affirming collective responsibility, the ethics of peace counter the atomised selfishness that lets the stronger flourish while the weaker go to the wall. It is often said that war offers people a heightened sense of community. In an age when we long for the community we have in so many ways done our best to destroy, war is stirringly and hideously collective. It does offer opportunities for heroism and self-sacrifice of the kind that helps people to create meaning out of existence. Surely we can devise creative channels for those attributes. The important thing is that they exist. They are a moral resource for the building of positive peace.

If we want the security that accompanies genuine democracy, a system that includes and respects all those who share a common territory, we need to work for its extension into international affairs. At present those of us who live in the West enjoy a measure of peace and democracy at home. We do not sanction, domestically, crude discrimination, we do not experience belief-based butchery or violence against children. Yet we project these inhumanities outwards into technological warfare in faraway places.

Just as war is a process, so is peace. Although it is important that we should think about where our choices may lead, the distinction that is often made between actions and outcomes is false. 'Consequences' are the things that follow on from where we have left off – or think we have. They are not a fixed state. They do not happen and then stop. Chaos theory and complexity theory[21] have, surely, made us a little more humble about our capacity to predict. How then are we to act responsibly? I believe we can do so only by doing things that are good in themselves and doing so on the basis of the best preparation we can manage, in terms of both understanding and imagination.

Whatever the dilemmas involved in rejecting mass violence, it makes no sense as a route to the kind of peace that is more than an episode in the cycle of war. And however negative it may seem to focus on the rejection of war, to deconstruct our belief in it is an essential step on the road to peace.[22] In the next chapter I shall explore the sources and forms of power for action against violence and for peace.

5
Opposing Evil and Standing Up for Good

Say No to peace
if what they mean by peace
is the quiet misery of hunger,
the frozen stillness of fear,
the silence of broken spirits,
the unborn hopes of the oppressed.

Tell them that peace
is the shouting of children at play,
the babble of tongues set free,
the thunder of dancing feet,
and a father's voice singing.

Brian Wren, *Say No to Peace*

Note that throughout history people have felt powerless before authority, but that at certain times these powerless people, by organizing, acting, risking, persisting, have created enough power to change the world around them, even if a little ... Remember, that those who have power and who seem invulnerable are in fact quite vulnerable, that their power depends on the obedience of others, and when those others begin withholding that obedience, begin defying authority, that power at the top turns out to be very fragile.

Howard Zinn, 'Staying the Course', 7 April 2003

Peace cannot be kept by force. It can only be achieved by understanding.

Albert Einstein

If the only tool you have is a hammer, you will see every problem as a nail.

Abraham Maslow

My argument so far has been that to oppose tyranny with counter-violence is to depend on and legitimise violent structures and technologies, to perpetuate the culture and cycle of violence. Any short-term benefits of war are vastly outweighed by its price in suffering and destruction and by the fact that every war gives new impetus to a system whose historic effects are already incomprehensibly terrible and whose future promises to be even more so. I have also argued that war is ethically indefensible and that its justification erodes the fundamental human values that are necessary to peace.

But that leaves us with a deep moral dilemma. Those values are daily abused by the violence of injustice, tyranny and aggression. Are we to stand by and do nothing? How are we to resist violent coercion without abandoning the ethics of peace? Does peacebuilding have to be abandoned in the face of violence? I will start with a question that encapsulates this dilemma.

WHAT ABOUT HITLER?

That is the question most often levelled at those who oppose any war, let alone war in general. Those who ask the question regard it as representing an argument of such power as to be unanswerable. Setting aside the fact that the parallel being drawn by the questioner is usually false, I think it is important to begin this discussion of alternatives with this recurrent challenge.

The first part of the response that should be made is that tyranny does not come from nowhere but is liable to take hold in certain conditions. Hitler, the child of a bullying father, was also the product of war. He was a particular manifestation of the culture of power, nationalism and violence, and the ground for his rise to power and for World War II was laid by World War I and the humiliating and punitive settlement imposed on Germany then. This, combined with subsequent policies of 'appeasement', prepared the way for Hitler's relentless pursuit of his ambitions.

The results of militarism and 'appeasement' cannot be laid at the door of those who opposed both. Nonetheless, how could the reality that manifested itself in the 1930s have been addressed? Do we have to accept that to engulf the world in a war that would fail to halt the killing of 6 million Jews and destroy 40 million lives was the best option available when Hitler marched into

Poland? Do we consider a success the establishment of a ruthless form of Communism across vast tracts of Europe? Are we happy with the arms race that ensued? Do we find ourselves living now in a world at peace? That is the negative side of the argument against the war that 'everyone' would support. But what, if any, were the other options?

At the point of high crisis in conflict, our options are certainly narrowed. Before and after war they are far greater. The relative room for manoeuvre has been pictured as an hourglass, wide at the top and bottom and tight in the middle.[1] In the years between the two world wars, for instance, in the light of the economic devastation of the German economy and its impact on the German people, those who had imposed the settlement could have modified it. European governments could have made vigorous representations to Hitler, challenging the direction of his policies while at the same time seeking to build positive relations with him and ease the plight of the people who were turning to him.

Hitler was ruthless and compelling, but even he depended on popular support for his power. That support could have been withheld and countered. At the grassroots level, a mass internationalist and anti-militarist movement could have been built and transnational solidarity networks developed. Such a movement could have supported those people in Germany and elsewhere who wanted to resist the rise of fascism, and could have put pressure on all European governments to support humane norms and values and build a new kind of international understanding. Supporting Germany's recovery and building such a movement would have required vision and commitment on the part of a great number of people but, given the will, would not have been impossible. Think of the scale of resources and commitment that go into building armies and fighting wars.

Given what did (and did not) happen, once Hitler's stranglehold on power had been established and his expansionist adventures had begun, what else could have been done but to fight? With the hourglass almost closed, was there anything different that could have been done? Though invasion had not been prevented, the possibilities for nonviolent resistance were many. As it was, in the countries that were occupied, civilisation did not die, though it was sorely challenged. There were many who upheld the values of freedom and equality. In one incident in Germany itself, in 1943, the wives and friends of Jews who had been taken from their homes gathered in their thousands outside the building where they had been locked up. Their protest was so vociferous and determined that 1,700 men were released – including many who had already been moved to the camps.

The Danish people under occupation, led by their king, practised nonviolent resistance, refusing to give up the Jews among them to the Nazis, wearing the Star of David as an act of solidarity. The Norwegians also resisted the orders of their occupiers and refused to teach Nazism in their schools. There was nonviolent (as well as violent) resistance to the German occupation of France, and many Jews there were sheltered in people's homes and saved from deportation, for instance by the villagers of Le Chambon, under the leadership of their pastor, André Trocme and his wife Magda.[2]

TYRANNY AND 'PEOPLE POWER'

These forms of resistance to Nazism were not organised in advance. They were simply the fruit of the moral integrity and courage of people living in the countries that Hitler's troops occupied. They may seem relatively insignificant in comparison to the scale of the war, but that is simply a reflection of the fact that nearly all our efforts, over recent millennia, have gone into our capacities for war, as against nonviolent forms of relationship and, where necessary, defence. Much thinking has since been devoted to the possibilities of systematic 'civilian-based' or 'social' defence.[3]

The coercive power of war is based on military capacity for destruction. The power of 'social defence' to resist coercion lies in the ultimate dependency of those who wish to control a society on the willingness of its members to be controlled. Nonviolent resistance means, primarily, non-cooperation with those who have taken power and autonomous action by the people in defiance of that power. It is effective when large numbers of people break ranks with the system that enthrals them and succeed in persuading some of those in key administrative or military positions to defect.

If we translated some of the key ideas of social defence and applied them, by way of illustration, to post-invasion Iraq, and the desire of many Iraqis to resist US occupation, we would see, for instance, instead of violent demonstrations and snipers picking off US troops and blowing up their vehicles:

- A concerted programme of non-cooperation with the occupying administration.
- Stay-at-homes by public servants.
- Strikes by oil workers.
- Persistent and growing public demonstrations, orderly and strictly nonviolent, so that any violence against them would bring global opprobrium on the occupying forces.
- The use of symbolism to communicate their message, locally and internationally, through the media.
- The establishment of parallel government systems – certainly at the local level – and 'unofficial' public services.
- The organisation of a rolling public debate about the future of Iraq, with the communication of emerging ideas and demands to the world at large and to the UN Secretary General.

Though there is some nonviolent resistance to the current occupation of Iraq, it is almost submerged in the violence. I believe that a concerted campaign of nonviolent resistance would not only have avoided the cruelty inflicted on Iraqis and foreign nationals alike: it would also have proved more effective than the widespread violence from multiple sources that has (at the time of writing) caused such suffering and constituted the main form of resistance. It would also have completed the moral isolation of the US.

It may be objected that such a programme would be impossible because different Iraqi factions, political or religious, would be unable or unwilling to work together. That may or may not be true. In the short term, in the face of an external enemy, societies can prove surprisingly united. A nonviolent campaign of resistance could have provided the focus for building a wide coalition and a vehicle for the development of public participation in rebuilding the country.

It may also be objected that we should be considering not how the Iraqi people could have rid themselves of the 'Coalition' occupiers but how they could have ousted Saddam Hussein. In fact the methods of resistance would be similar, but the psychological context very different. A tyranny that has been in place for a long time and been maintained through systematic brutality is indeed very difficult to counter. However, it is not by any means impossible – it has been done.

Whether tyrannies come from without or within, by nature they concentrate power in very few hands. To function, they depend on the compliance – and work – of the mass of the population and to achieve this they rely heavily on intimidation, maintained by sporadic atrocities and the climate of fear that they engender. While this strategy can prove remarkably effective, the position of tyrants is always vulnerable. The first step is to begin to establish, however secretly, an alternative discourse to the one that has been imposed.[4] The next step is to recognise the collective power of the population. The third is for courageous individuals to take action and begin to encourage others to do the same.

Resistance need not, initially, take the form of open defiance. It can be expressed through actions and choices that are 'normal' and legal, even in tyrannies – like being ill on the same day as others, so that workplaces are incapacitated; or failing one's exams deliberately and being unable to take up a certain kind of work; or taking one's car out at the same time as others and driving rather slowly and clogging up the roads; or turning on all one's electrical appliances at a given time and helping to bring the country to a standstill.

In a society that has suffered for a long time from violent repression, it is hard to break the silence and fear that induce complicity. The primary ingredient is a few people with imagination and courage who dare to initiate concerted action – or inaction – either by word of mouth or by some swift and courageous stand to trigger a change in public mood.

I remember listening enthralled, many years ago, to a friend from Uruguay, who bore the marks of torture on his body but who had undertaken a public fast with two fellow-priests against the then dictatorship. On the final day of their fast, at the time when they had announced that it would end, all the people went into their streets and yards and banged their pots and pans for several minutes. This cacophony was followed by a two-minute silent stoppage, which brought factories and traffic to a standstill. This show of strength and exercise of 'voice' was prepared by word of mouth along streets where everyone knew someone who had been tortured or 'disappeared'. It heralded the end of the dictatorship. A crescendo of public protest forced the dictatorship to call a general election and the military junta was replaced with a civilian government.

Not only can tyrants be overthrown nonviolently: since any potential invader needs the recognition and acquiescence – at least – of a population it seeks to govern, it is reasonable to suppose that the knowledge that a country's population was thoroughly prepared to resist the rule of an invader would constitute a powerful deterrent. As the US has learned to its cost, winning a war is not the same as 'winning the peace', and well-developed and advertised plans to prevent that victory should make any invader think twice.

NONVIOLENT RESISTANCE IN RECENT HISTORY

The fact that empires have been built demonstrates the weakness of conventional military defence against invasion by bigger powers. At the same time, a review of history suggests that unwilling populations cannot be subjugated indefinitely. Even the staying power of the mightiest of armies may be matched and eventually overcome by the tenacity of resistance to occupation, whether violent or nonviolent.

The anti-colonial campaign of Mohandas Gandhi[5] against the British was astounding in its size, discipline and success. It is sometimes argued (by British people) that it worked only because the British were so 'civilised', but anyone who saw the film *Gandhi* or read accounts of the massacre at Amritsar will dismiss that objection.

Many years ago in Johannesburg, I met a pacifist anti-apartheid clergyman (Rob Robertson) who had made a comparative study of Gandhi's nonviolent campaign to rid India of British rule and of the war led by Ahmed Ben Bella to free Algeria from France. His research was never published, but it revealed that while Ben Bella's war was concluded a little more quickly than Gandhi's campaign, the number of deaths involved was very much higher. The broader legacy must also have been very different, though violence continued to mar life in both countries and their respective regions.

For a long time the triumph of nonviolence in India seemed to stand as a somewhat isolated example of what could be done on such a scale. When, at the beginning of the 1990s the collapse of the Soviet empire was achieved in a remarkably short time and almost entirely without violence (even with very few deaths of protesters), our whole understanding of power and who holds it should have changed. The dependence of any regime on popular submission was demonstrated in the most dramatic and powerful way.

It is worth noting that the movement whose rapid and astonishing rise resulted in the demise of Communism in Europe was built on the 'failed' insurrections of the past – notably the East German uprising in 1953, the Hungarian uprising in 1956 and the Prague Spring of 1968. There was also a continuity of ideas, networks and individuals through the 1960s and 1970s.[6] Dissidents continued to promote ideas of freedom, often using the churches as a venue for ongoing debate. In some cases they were supported by the peace movements in the West.

The birth and growth of Solidarnosc (Solidarity) in Poland, in 1980–81, as a trade union and eventually as a political party, marked a turning point. The final collapse of Communism began in Poland, with the strikes and mass demonstrations organised by members of Solidarnosc, along with the group named Freedom and Peace. In Hungary there was an accelerating process of government reforms and popular action, from 1987 on, culminating in the approval of a multi-party system in the autumn of 1989. In the same year a 'velvet revolution' took place in Czechoslovakia, with thousands rallying in Prague's Wenceslas Square, holding torches into the night. And in East Germany the persistence of a broad-based peace movement led to the resignation of Erik Honecker and the fall of the Berlin Wall. Communist rule in Bulgaria came to an end in the same year and on 25 December the Ceausescus were executed in Romania, in an otherwise peaceful revolution.[7]

The Baltic states, 'given' to Russia after World War II, were next in line. There again, courageous individuals led a vast popular uprising. A small number were killed by government forces before these were overwhelmed and conceded defeat, but the changes came about with remarkably few deaths. Russia itself began to see the old regime's control lifted under Mikhail Gorbachev, and citizens poured into the space that he had created. Spectacular confrontations between tanks and demonstrators and the storming of the Duma (Russian parliament) saw the old Communist regime defeated. (The public humiliation of Gorbachev by Boris Yeltsin at the end of this operation was one of the less edifying moments in the process.)

As I write, a 'velvet revolution' has just taken place in Georgia, removing Eduard Shevardnadze from power after an election victory which was generally believed to have been rigged. It is ironic that someone who played such a positive role as Gorbachev's Foreign Secretary and later as the post-Soviet President of Georgia should himself fall victim to 'people power'. And in this case, as in those of the past, it is easy to see that 'people power' can be used for different motives and may not necessarily herald in good governments and global solutions.[8] Still it is important to digest the salient fact that governments rely on the acquiescence of those they govern, and that the armies and police forces they employ to defend them and maintain their power are themselves people whose allegiance may change. That the nature and scale of these staggering events made so little difference to our attitude to war and its alternatives bears witness to the power and longevity of the myth, culture and structures of violence.

In fact, the new phenomenon of 'people power' that brought down the Soviet empire had already made its appearance (and acquired its name) far away in the Philippines, where the persistence and courage of the organisers and the crowds brought about the ousting of the despotic President Marcos in 1986. General Ramos was confronted by the people who had blocked the streets of Manila but refused to advance against them. He and his men defected and the dictator fled.

Though religion is often seen as encouraging war and colluding with state powers, in the Philippines, as in Eastern Europe, the churches played a significant role in providing both inspiration and an organising framework for collective nonviolent action for liberation. The image of nuns carrying crosses, sitting in front of tanks in Manila and offering the soldiers food, flowers and cigarettes, became a potent symbol of the power of nonviolence.

In 1989 similarly stirring images from China of students in Tiananmen Square in Beijing, defiantly standing in front of tanks, reached the world. This time, however, the tanks rolled over the students – an ugly reminder that nonviolent opposition, like violent resistance, can fail at a given time and can have a heavy price. The failure of this uprising also pointed to the importance of organisation and of building popular support – which the student movement had not done. The combination of their uncompromising demands and the relatively puny size and isolation of their movement made their success unlikely. And yet they *were* successful, in that their courage remains an inspiration. The memory of the lone student's defiance will outlive the tanks and their drivers. China will not be able to resist change indefinitely.

After the staggering events of the late 1980s and early 1990s, the next world event that should have confounded our fixed notions of power was the collapse of the 'apartheid' regime in South Africa. What had begun as a nonviolent campaign under the leadership of Albert Luthuli, and 'diversified' with the setting up of the ANC's armed wing after the Sharpeville massacre, was eventually brought to fruition by the unarmed insurrection of the people of the townships – starting with the schoolchildren and their boycotts, followed by rent boycotts and economic boycotts (of stores, for instance) and the 'relentless persistence'[9] of mass demonstrations (often on the occasion of funerals, turning defeat into the triumph of defiance). Though the Afrikaans churches supported apartheid for a long time, the churches in general played a vital role in inspiring and supporting their members in resistance to it. (The pacifist clergyman who carried out the Gandhi–Ben Bella study led a church that at any given time had several of its members in detention.) And although Nelson Mandela, who was freed in 1994, was imprisoned for planning violence against the state, the story of his life as a prisoner on Robben Island is one of magnanimity, human outreach and forgiveness. He has become a hero not of guerrilla warfare but of reconciliation.

PEOPLE POWER AROUND THE WORLD

It seemed important to recount this staggering sequence of events that has demonstrated beyond all doubt the capacity of people power to effect regime change, because it convincingly refutes the established view that only military power is able to resist and overthrow tyranny. Now I want to give some illustrations from around the world to show that nonviolent resistance and action for change have a much wider history, spanning continents.

To start in the Middle East, the situation in Israel–Palestine mirrors in many ways the relationships that for so long disfigured South Africa. On a recent visit to Jerusalem and the West Bank I watched a video about nonviolent resistance in Africa.[10] The scenes of tanks entering the townships to crush rebellions there were strikingly similar to scenes of tanks in the towns and villages of the occupied Palestinian territories. In the first 'Intifada' or uprising, violence was minimal. The power of the movement lay in the determination of an apparently powerless people in standing up to military occupation. The sight of youngsters with stones facing up to soldiers with machine guns and tanks was a symbol of naked courage more than of violence. Though it certainly was not emblematic of principled nonviolence, it did demonstrate the power of non-military resistance, and because of the contrast between the military power of the Israelis and the unarmed defiance of the resisters it won strong sympathy for the Palestinian cause. It seems reasonable to suppose that this contributed much to creating the international interest and will to see that a settlement of the conflict should be reached.

The new Intifada that followed the subsequent violations and collapse of the Oslo Peace Accord (in particular the continued expansion of the settlements), and which was finally triggered by the provocative actions of Ariel Sharon, was focused more on armed movements than on the basic, unarmed resistance of a population. Their activities have included both the targeted killing of soldiers and settlers and the indiscriminate killing of Israeli citizens by suicide bombers. This has enabled Israel to point constantly to its need for self-defence in justifying its own repressive violence. The resort by some to violent means has given Israeli hawks the advantage by entering the military arena in which the Israeli army excels. That is why, whenever there has been a ceasefire in the offing from one of the armed Palestinian groups, a major act of provocation – such as an assassination involving the blowing up of homes – has been arranged to derail it. A ceasefire would not to be to the advantage of those who seek to crush the Palestinians rather than seek accommodation with them.

Latin America offers a wealth of examples of both violent and nonviolent resistance to tyranny. Across the continent people have struggled for social justice and for freedom from political tyranny and rampant militarism. Typically, tyranny and insurrections coexisted for decades, with ordinary people caught in the crossfire between repressive, right-wing governments and the guerrilla forces opposing them. Political violence, disappearance and death squads enforced the control of dictators and mafias, while the majority of the people lived in desperate poverty. Indigenous peoples have suffered greatly. At the social level the machismo culture has added domestic and street violence to the misery endured.

At the same time, people's resilience and courage, their capacity for solidarity, and the commitment of so many to social justice in the face of such gross inequality have been an inspiration to the global nonviolence movement. In Uruguay, as we have seen, a nonviolent uprising ousted a dictatorship. In Ecuador indigenous people have struggled nonviolently to win back the legal right to the land which was taken from them and given to multinational corporations. They have made some progress in winning back their rights. In Argentina, the mothers of the Plaza de Mayo campaigned tirelessly on behalf of the 'disappeared' and brought the extent of human rights crimes to light. In Chile and Guatemala the move from military to civilian regimes was eventually achieved through persistent popular action. In Bolivia the government has recently been forced out of office by the scale of public protests.

Not that peace and justice now reign supreme in Latin America! There is a long way to go. Colombia is wracked with violence and its people squeezed between a violent government, funded by the US, and the FARC guerrillas. In former dictatorships the crimes of the past have not been adequately addressed. The international business mafia is curtailing the powers of governments to address the needs of their people. Nonetheless, most of the advances that have been made have been the fruit more of civilian, unarmed action than of guerrilla activity. (The notable exceptions are Nicaragua and Cuba. Given the cost of their wars – moral, physical, psychological and political – and the current situation in Cuba, it must be worth asking whether nonviolence would not have been a better choice for them too.) And now in Brazil it seems that a real alternative is emerging – a form of democracy that really is focused on the wellbeing of the people.

Much of the continent of Africa, ravaged by colonialism, has since been held back by exploitative international trading systems and greedy corporations, its own corrupt leaders, covert political and military intervention from outside and home-grown factionalism. The results have been poverty, violence and forced migration on an epic scale. Yet, quite apart from the overthrow of apartheid in South Africa, other African countries offer many heroic examples of people power in action. In Nigeria, nonviolent action has been used to resist environmental destruction by oil companies. In Sierra Leone, when the violence was at its height and dissident voices were unwelcome to the government, women built a substantial, public movement for peace and the Council of Churches acted as mediators. In Wajir, in Kenya, women, tribal leaders and young people acted to address inter-communal violence. In Somalia, a traditional council of clan elders worked to address inter-clan tensions and violence. In Zimbabwe, opposition leaders and their supporters have braved the most brutal violence and refused to give up their efforts to see Robert Mugabe removed from office.

Asia, too, offers a wealth of experience in people power, though it is often lost in the welter of more negative realities. Resistance to totalitarianism in China continues, for instance through the courageous defiance of Falun Gong practitioners and human rights activists. In the run-up to the end of British (autocratic) rule in Hong Kong, the democracy movement played an important role in ensuring that human rights and political liberties would be protected there, to some degree at least, once the island was returned to China. In India, Gandhian organisations are active in movements for ecological protection and in nonviolent intervention to protect lives and build bridges in the face of violent Hindu nationalism and the tensions it has created. In Sri Lanka and Nepal, many activists are working to promote dialogue and offer alternatives to civil war.

Though violent separatist movements had long been (and remain) active in several European countries, our continent had for many years been relatively free of large-scale political violence, until wars began to erupt in the countries where the old Communist regimes had been brought down. The wars in what was Yugoslavia have attracted the most attention in the West since they are the closest. Many individuals and groups resisted the build-up to war in that region but failed to prevent it.

They did, however, create another kind of reality alongside it: a network of people working in a very different direction, opposing the war and resisting the creation of newly antagonistic relationships between people of different ethnic backgrounds. They came together in groups that were themselves ethnically mixed. They held public protests and did what they could to protect those they knew were under threat from vigilantes or the military. They lived their beliefs as well as advocating them. They developed programmes of education for tolerance and nonviolence and helped refugees to manage their lives in exile. They built a network of friendship and solidarity across the region and somehow managed the tensions which that entailed, keeping peace alive in the midst of war. And when the war ended, their groups and networks constituted a vibrant resource for the slow and arduous process of rebuilding relationships, coming to terms with the past and beginning to establish the values and practices of respect and participation. In Serbia, a movement built on the nonviolent expertise that had been amassed before, during and since the war eventually accomplished the removal of President Milosevic from power in a spectacular demonstration of strategic people power.

In what used to be called 'Western Europe', and in other 'Western' countries, there is a tradition of nonviolent resistance – to war, nuclear weapons, economic globalisation, ecological threats and so on. In the United States of America, whose military capacity is – literally – astronomical, nonviolent resistance has a strong and inspiring history. The US Civil Rights Movement of the 1950s and 1960s was remarkable, effective (as far as it went) and inspiring.[11] The speeches and writings of Martin Luther King and many others strengthened the philosophical grounding of the global nonviolence movement. There is now, as then, a strong radical movement in the US, committed and adept in the use of different forms of nonviolent action and civil disobedience.[12]

THE STRENGTH OF NONVIOLENCE – BUILDING PEACE

When people in Britain reminisce about World War II, they are often nostalgic about the sense of solidarity that it evokes: the way in which people 'did their bit' and 'pulled together'. They compare this sadly with what they see as today's selfish, atomised society. Civilian-based defence requires both a sense of individual responsibility and the feeling – and reality – of 'pulling together'. Personal commitment and collective action are two sides of the same coin. The central idea of nonviolent or civilian defence is to make a people self-reliant in the face of tyranny – able to resist it not by countering it in kind but by withholding co-operation and exercising the right to autonomy. This power of refusal is complemented by the power of communication and persuasion. The goal is not conquest but the overcoming of violence and enmity.

Nonviolence has nothing to do with inaction or passivity. The fact that it does not kill people or destroy the earth is, in itself, certainly an enormous advantage. But it offers, positively, both a means of combating violence and injustice and, at the same time, of upholding and strengthening the values and practices of peace. Nonviolence is peace and democracy in action, while war is the opposite. War is the exercise of lethal power by a certain section of society at the behest of a few powerful people, who take decisions behind closed doors. The power of nonviolence comes from a broad base, from the 'weak' as well as the 'strong'. It is founded in popular participation, both in decision-making and in action. It relies on all kinds of qualities – analysis, imagination, courage, persistence and the power to communicate. It can use all kinds and all levels of contribution.

Essentially, nonviolence depends on the will of individual human beings to take up their own power and responsibility to act with others for the things they believe in – just as organised violence depends on the participation of individual human beings. Both can call for great courage – but that is one of the positive values celebrated in war. In Idi Amin's Uganda, while some people were following the dictator's orders to kill their fellow citizens in their homes, others were giving neighbours shelter and refusing entry to those who would murder them. In Israel today, an increasing number of young men and women refuse to do their military service and act in solidarity with Palestinians who are under attack. There is always a choice.

But peace is more than the absence of war and tyranny. 'Positive peace' requires a continuous process of building and maintenance, which, if it were carried out, would remove the causes of war. The turbulence and violence that followed the collapse of Communism in Europe and Eurasia are a sad demonstration of the fact that removing dictatorships, even nonviolently, is far easier than building peace. Those who had put their all into ending a system had apparently not thought out, conceptually or strategically, the alternative that should replace it. The countries that have experienced the least difficulty in that regard have been those at the periphery of the former Soviet empire, later additions to it, that had stronger democratic traditions and where the change from opposition to government – however dramatic – was part of an ongoing process for those involved.

Achieving genuine and lasting peace means transforming societies. It involves addressing not only immediate behaviour and attitudes but the whole context in which people think and act, including the prevailing culture, social patterns, and political and economic systems. Preventing or stopping a war or removing a tyrant is one step on a long road, and even societies that face no such dramatic challenge may nonetheless need to be transformed. 'Reality' is confined to what happens in the big arena, the national stage. It is also what is done in a particular home or school, factory or village.

And even where people's action seems to fail, with hindsight they can be seen to have sown the seeds of peace.

Our participation, then, is necessary to peace and fundamental to nonviolent options. Peace is not something that is bestowed on us, still less imposed on us – or on anyone else – from outside. It is something we create and work on where we live. It is the job of all people in all countries. We need to develop the will and the skills that are necessary for peacebuilding work, at whatever stage and of whatever kind: resistance, advocacy of all kinds, bridge-building, mediation, education, building movements or 'constituencies' for peace, participating in peace processes and negotiations, institution-building, and more general social and political participation.

INTERNATIONAL SOLIDARITY

If nonviolent resistance to violence and tyranny is essentially the task of local people, do we have no responsibility to intervene on their behalf? What about the terrible internal wars that have ravaged so many countries – in the former Yugoslavia, in many former Soviet territories, in Sri Lanka, Indonesia, Sudan, the Congo, Israel–Palestine. Is there nothing we can do to stop them?

Within the prevailing military system, some of these wars have raged for decades before eventually giving way to an uneasy 'peace'. Others continue unabated or have flared up repeatedly. Yet others have 'frozen', without victory or resolution, and continue to threaten weary and impoverished populations, keeping displaced people in limbo.

The warring parties in these conflicts would no doubt argue that their struggle is also motivated by justice, or the need to deal with enemies of the state, or the right to maintain territorial integrity. In Rwanda, the Hutus who instigated the murder of so many Tutsis claimed to have been dominated by them for too long. In Sri Lanka, those living in the Tamil-dominated North argued that the only way for them to obtain what they needed was by gaining independence from the Sinhala-dominated South. In Sierra Leone, those who took up arms against their government and fought with such brutality gained support on the basis that it was time for the many that were marginalised and dispossessed to have a leadership that would meet their needs. But those of us who watch from afar, though in some cases we may sympathise with a particular cause, are shocked by the carnage and long to see some action to end it. When wars are seen at a distance, and without any vested interest, they are seen for the disaster that they are.

As we have seen, justifications for war on humanitarian grounds are persuasive. Even if the claimed motives are not genuine, we are left with a serious question about the nature and boundaries of human solidarity, which sits side by side with empowerment and autonomy at the heart of nonviolence. If we are not to rely on the methods and structures of violence, how are we to respond? This question has exercised nonviolent activists for many decades.

Yet the reality is that most wars (and tyrannies) run their course without any interruption from the big powers. (As noted earlier, in a recent radio interview a senior EU politician declared that it was inconceivable that military action would be taken to overthrow the despotic regime in Myanmar/Burma).[13] The reluctance of the US to send troops to Liberia was put down to the drain on its military resources resulting from its entanglement in Afghanistan and Iraq. Even the mightiest power has its limits and most civil wars attract rather little attention from the 'international community'. Some low-level diplomatic and NGO (non-governmental organisation) activity may be supported, but no more than that.

The hourglass metaphor applies here, too. While conflict is at its height, options are limited for militarism and nonviolence alike. Unless they are to enter a war on the side of one party (as happened in the case of Kosovo) external forces can come in as 'peacekeepers' only once a ceasefire is more or less in place.

Are the populations of violent regions simply to sit and wait for the dubious benefit of invasion? It seems neither feasible nor desirable that 'peace' in currently violent regions should depend on the armed might of a few powerful nations. Quite apart from the impossibility of organising military intervention on so many fronts, such a model offers no real autonomy, dignity or democracy and therefore no real peace. Not only does it perpetuate the system and culture of militarism but, as we in the UK have found from our experience in Northern Ireland, civil conflict cannot be resolved by violence, be it the violence of 'terrorists' or national armies or anyone else, and solutions cannot be imposed from outside.

The only way for such situations to be transformed is through a long and arduous process of community development, education, dialogue, mediation and negotiation, confidence-building and co-operation. Political solutions have to be found and re-found. Those pushed to the margins of society have to be given a place within it. Past wrongs must be acknowledged, reparations made and lines drawn. The difficulties are enormous. They are not diminished by constant resort to violence, but they can be reduced by support of all kinds to the local people who have to address them – moral, financial and technical.

Non-governmental organisations and individuals from outside, whether volunteers or professionals, can also help local actors engaged in the business of overcoming injustice, resolving conflict or building peace. They can do so through moral support – by visits, email exchanges, postal links, twinnings and so on; by sharing skills and information, and by facilitating dialogue or acting as advocates. They can also help by alerting solidarity networks and human rights organisations (such as Amnesty International) and their own governments when people are in specific danger and may be saved by international attention and diplomatic pressure.

Although the principles of empowerment and autonomy are at the heart of nonviolence, so is solidarity. Certainly at present we do not take this seriously enough. Jo Wilding, a peace activist living in Iraq, has been talking to local people about their attitude to the invasion and occupation of their country, which the majority of them opposes. She gives a sobering account of the chronic intimidation and informing, the constant and gross human rights violations which over many years attracted very little solidarity action. And, describing the terrible impact of international sanctions on people's daily lives and the way in which they helped keep Saddam Hussein in power, she notes that international protests against these sanctions were small in scale – unlike the demonstrations against the war. She argues that those of us who live in safety have to face up to our responsibilities for those who do not:

> We need to get out more. We need to pull down more statues, blockade more corporations, shout louder, more often and more consistently, demand an end to our governments' support for any leaders and governments which don't respect human rights. We need to learn a lesson in destruction of the mental constructs that say there's nothing we can do, take the risks ... Then maybe we'll understand solidarity.[14]

Not only is solidarity action needed at a distance but, since Gandhi's time, there has been a concern among groups and individuals committed to nonviolence to find ways for self-organised civilians to contribute directly to the prevention of violence through nonviolent intervention. For many years Peace Brigades International (PBI) has sent trained volunteers to accompany nonviolent activists who are in danger, to enable them to continue their own resistance to violence.[15]

For instance, when the leadership of the mothers of disappeared people in Guatemala were being murdered one by one, PBI volunteers went to live with them and never left them unguarded, day or night. Though they carried no weapons, their presence and the international attention that it brought helped to reduce the extreme vulnerability of the women. And when the worst violence was over and refugees wanted to return to their homes, teams of PBI volunteers accompanied them, to make their journey safer and to support them as they returned to their villages.

In spring 2003, human shields went to Iraq to try to deter the threatened war. They failed to do so, but their presence was hugely appreciated by those they met and they played a valuable role in sending first-hand information back to their home countries. Currently an international nonviolent presence is providing some much needed protection and solidarity to Palestinians, as well as supporting Israeli peace groups and facilitating dialogue.

All these small, non-governmental contributions have real practical value. I would suggest that, on a much larger scale and given a level of commitment comparable to that currently made to military options, such interventions could make a very great difference. Since such means have been seen as peripheral, they have been starved of resources. Given the political will, this could change and bring about a revolution in the way 'intervention' is thought about.

A CONSTRUCTIVE ROLE FOR GOVERNMENTS IN SUPPORTING PEACE 'ABROAD'

Most of this chapter has been about the power of ordinary people to resist abuses of power and to bring about radical change. That is because 'people power' is the key to peace and democracy. However, it is important not to overlook the constructive, nonviolent options open to governments and those who design foreign policy. Despite the continuing prevalence of militarism, some small but positive shifts have taken place in recent years.

Already some countries are beginning to shift their approach to foreign affairs, moving away from the old emphasis on military preparedness and intervention, and towards constructive intervention (such as genuine mediation) and support for local capacities for peace. With the exception of Costa Rica, none has entirely demilitarised its foreign policy, but many put far more emphasis now on international co-operation, support and influence, and far less on bullying and threats. These countries base their policy on the notion of common security rather than relying on dominance. The EU's policy, for all its faults, is in part at least an experiment in this approach.

The first thing external governments can do is to honour and support local activists who are working to address violence within their society – whether they do so directly or via a non-governmental organisation working in solidarity with them. They should do this not only when it serves their own national interests but as a matter of principle. Some governments with the capacity to do this – for instance, Canada, the Netherlands and Scandinavian countries – offer substantial support in this way to activists working for democracy and against violence of whatever kind. Even in the UK some progress is being made – a small undertow in the bigger, continuing tide of militarism. A new, interdepartmental 'Global Prevention Fund' has been established to support 'civil society' initiatives, in countries where conflict is – or could become – violent. The scope and responsiveness of such initiatives are, however, woefully inadequate and they are too closely tied to self-serving agendas, such as maintaining a manageable environment for investment and exploitation of natural resources.

One recent experience of mine will illustrate the inadequacy of current capacities for peace. Not so long ago I was involved in some 'off-the-record' meetings with small groups of people, in particular circles of Palestinian political leadership who wished to explore and develop new forms of nonviolent action. They needed to find ways of acting that would at once uphold Palestinian dignity and rights and allow them to escape from a dynamic in which they would always be the losers and which perpetuated the fears of Israeli Jews – and therefore their support for Ariel Sharon. They were looking for support and expertise, as a matter of urgency, and their needs were known to European governments. Yet no financial and organisational base was found to support such work. Armies stand ready to fight all over the world, but modest and timely support for nonviolence is not yet readily at hand. That needs to change.

Non-military assistance can be given not only to non-governmental groups but also by one government to another, in the shape of support of every kind for building peace – whether before widespread political violence has erupted (both for the sake of 'positive peace' and in order to prevent war) or after war has happened. Such assistance can include support in building institutions and developing or rebuilding a country's infrastructure and economy.

As Dr Hanan Ashrawi put it recently,[16] 'The nature of pre-emptive action must be, by necessity and choice, constructive, peaceful and therapeutic'. One therapeutic contribution is to offer 'good offices'. The arts of genuine, facilitative mediation (as against the 'power mediation' or strong-arming of, for instance, the US) are being developed and put to good use by countries like Norway, which played a key role in helping Palestinians and Israelis to initiate a peace process (now sadly defunct). More recently it also played a key role in brokering a ceasefire in Sri Lanka and chairing negotiations between the government and the LTTE (Liberation Tigers of Tamil Eelam). Such help can be vital. Finding more ways to strengthen and validate such processes by drawing in 'civil society' will be a vital next step in the development of such mediatory capacities.

The skills for this kind of activity need to be developed. If governments are serious about them they will put resources into training, preparing their own citizens for such supportive and constructive intervention – as well as for nonviolent political engagement at home and for nonviolent resistance.

Being willing to supply and support peacekeepers in situations where violent conflict has been brought to a halt is another way in which governments can contribute to creating a situation in which peacebuilding can begin. Peacekeepers need to be trained for a policing rather than a fighting role. Better still, they could *be* police rather than soldiers. If the world is to be demilitarised, that will be part of the process.

The establishment of the Organization for Security and Co-operation in Europe (OSCE) to develop ways of intervening constructively in conflict and to prevent or end related violence can be seen as a step in the right direction. The OSCE began its life as a Conference (the CSCE) which was in reality an ongoing forum for dialogue between East and West when they were highly polarised blocs. It embraces Canada and the US, the whole of the former Soviet Union and the whole of Europe.

The OSCE's main function is still to offer to participating states the constant possibility of dialogue, so helping to address tensions and build trust and co-operation. It also engages in 'early warning' of potential conflicts and 'preventive diplomacy' in response to such warnings. It contributes to 'positive peace' by helping participating states to fulfil their commitments to human rights, democracy and the rule of law.[17] It has established long-term field missions in Bosnia-Herzegovina, Estonia, Georgia and Tajikistan. Its activities include making representations to governments in support of human rights; supplying mediators to help in the search for the political settlement of disputes; sending teams of observers to make reports on given situations and processes (such as ceasefires or elections), exercising political and moral pressure by their presence and the implied attention of other countries; providing monitors to act as active supervisors of agreed processes; supplying civilian police in certain situations and providing training for the many civilian roles necessary to the establishment of social stability and political participation.

In addition to giving political, diplomatic and financial support for local civil resistance, governments have the means to engage directly with a 'regime' that oppresses its own people or threatens the security of others. They have options that do not involve killing large numbers of that country's population; that uphold, rather than undermine, international democracy. Such options involve consulting and acting with others rather than unilaterally, and seeking agreement rather than preferring to dictate. Governments bring the collective will to bear on a situation and can involve similar elements to those that compose the nonviolent repertoire of their citizens: advocacy and support for change and a refusal to collude with the status quo by suspending co-operation. But in addition they have an option which citizens do not have: that of substantial inducements. Instead of relying on their power to inflict damage, they can focus on their capacity to support and offer incentives.

Slobodan Milosevic – who was eventually removed not by war but by popular action – might have been induced to change his ways, if Western governments had supported local pressure by offering him incentives to change, rather than forcing him into a corner and launching a war against his country – a war not supported by those who later removed him.

Early in 2003, a couple of months before the war on Iraq was launched, I was a panellist at a public meeting where someone in the audience asked us all what we thought could be done to turn Saddam Hussein from an enemy into a friend. The question sounded naïve, but it produced some interesting answers. Revisiting the question now, I remain convinced of its wisdom in shifting the focus of our discussion away from threat and counter-threat to positive alternatives that could change the dynamic of hostility.

Saddam Hussein could have been dealt with in other ways – if the liberation and wellbeing of Iraqis and global security had been the real cause for concern, and the agenda for change that was promoted had indeed had international backing. External pressure and, particularly, positive incentives, could have created a space for internal civil action. Academic exchange could have begun to open up society to other energies and influences, supporting change. The lifting of sanctions would have eased the misery of the people and at the same time reduced passive support for the regime. Rebuilding the country's infrastructure would have restored morale and economic prosperity. If the making of conditions had been presented in a face-saving way, such a deal could have moved things forward for all concerned. Such a deal could even have included the deployment of human rights monitors.[18]

Working with despots and 'the men of violence' is an uneasy option, but it is constantly being done – as it was in Northern Ireland. Whatever the means used to end violence and tyranny, hard judgements have to be made about the balance to be struck between the need to end violence and the need for justice. In theory, positive peace includes justice, but in making the transition from war (or the threat of it) to the beginning of the long road to peace, a trade-off may need to be made. Bringing an end to immediate tyranny or carnage is a necessary and urgent step if justice and peace are to have any kind of a chance.

In Chapter 2, I suggested that dignity and honour were important motivators for politicians – and human beings generally, especially so in non-Western cultures. When Western politicians set out to humiliate particular governments (quite apart from any general crassness and insensitivity) they not only destroy any likelihood of having some constructive influence on them but they alienate large sectors of the world's population, thereby losing the possibility of concerted support for change. There is a difference between plain speaking and insults, and there are appropriate contexts and channels for communication. Our diplomats know this and have appropriate training and skills. Our politicians seem to have been trained in another school.

The arrogance of the West is particularly galling because it demands of others rules of conduct it does not itself adhere to. This is most blatant in the matter of security. No one is to threaten the West but the West can threaten everyone else. What about those Iraqi weapons of mass destruction – had they ever existed? Undoubtedly they once did, but the inspection regime had apparently been effective in eliminating them. However that may be, the answer to the WMD threat is much broader and more profound. It goes to the heart of what is wrong with international relations and with the role ascribed to itself by the West.

Only when we look at ourselves and put our own house in order will we have any moral authority in the world. Only when we adhere to our own side of the nuclear Non-proliferation Treaty – to tackle, urgently, the task of getting rid of our own nuclear weapons – will we have the right to demand that others do the same. Only when we begin to behave democratically in international relations, rather than wielding the big sticks of economic and military dominance, will we have the right to preach democracy.

AN ANSWER TO TERRORISM?

Does nonviolence provide an answer to terrorism? No more of an answer, in the short term, than violence. But at least it is not a constant provocation to it, a pretext for it, or a different version of it. Nonviolence upholds the value of justice that terrorism, like other forms of organised violence, so often claims as its goal. It offers another way of addressing structural violence and working for dignity and respect.

The religious motivations which many terrorists claim for what they do will not be removed but strengthened by violence against them, which is the stimulus for fanaticism as well as its fruit. (This applies to fanatics of all religions and none.) Such movements thrive on opposition. How can their hold on hearts and minds be weakened? What else can fill the space that they have occupied in societies and in movements?

Transformation is needed not only in the hearts and minds of terrorists but in the way in which powerful 'democratic' governments understand and exercise power. To threaten the world with vast armies, fearful weaponry and massive nuclear arsenals is also to terrorise. To believe that your own way of doing things is so superior as to warrant this threat is another sort of fanaticism.

The violence of war is mirrored and fuelled by the cruel attitudes and daily brutality that are present in so many societies and systems. The scourge of poverty is a daily affront to humanity, and the habitats of human beings and other species are ravaged for the enrichment of the few. None of us escapes involvement in the myriad forms of violence – economic, political and environmental – that militarism reflects and enforces.

Western 'democracies' have espoused the values of the 'Enlightenment' and to varying degrees put them into practice – in their (relative) respect for the rule of law, for human rights and democratic processes.[19] To recognise that the United States and others have so patently and increasingly flouted these norms in recent times is not to deny the fact that most of us would prefer the relative day-to-day safety and social provision of most Western countries to the levels of inequality, danger and political malpractice suffered by the majority of people in so many parts of the world. These – and war and poverty – are the miseries that drive so many people to flee their own countries and seek refuge in the West.

Yet the West has projected its own forms of violence outwards on to the rest of the world: the violence of economic exploitation and political hegemony, enforced by military might (including weapons of mass destruction). And increasingly that might is being concentrated into the hands of a single superpower – arguably the one most corrupted by its own power for dominance.

PEOPLE POWER TO RESIST MILITARISM AND DEMAND PEACE

The culture of violence, and our reliance on it as a mechanism for dealing with differences and gaining control over one another, has brought us to a point where militarism itself constitutes the world's greatest tyranny, devastating lives and land, forcing mass migrations, preventing development and prosperity. Whoever we are and wherever we live, we have a role to play – whether we are motivated by our own present suffering, or distressed by what we see happening to others and fearful for the wider future of humanity. The system of war and domination that could annihilate our planet is a tyranny we all need to confront. It is clear that war cannot be abolished by violence. It is also clear that the existence of a military system is the most fundamental obstacle to peace. This, then, is an overriding challenge to people power.

The examples I have given of nonviolent action around the world are taken from countries experiencing immediate violence or repression. Nonviolent action in Western democracies is more often focused on the policies and actions of their own governments that violate the needs and rights of people in other countries and consume resources needed for public services at home. For many decades now the anti-militarist movement has ebbed and flowed. Its members have been responsible for many brave and imaginative actions, in city centres and at nuclear installations, outside government buildings and on bomber-base runways. This Western anti-war movement (closely aligned to the movement for global justice) has grown in recent times and found common cause with anti-war protesters on every continent. When the US and UK launched their war on Iraq, millions of people across the world cared enough and made enough effort to organise and demonstrate against it.

Many people go on supporting war because they can think of no alternative form of power. I have tried to show that 'people power' offers a real alternative; that, if it were taken seriously and organised systematically, it could make military defence obsolete. It would at the same time transfer power from the few to the many. Perhaps that is why it is unattractive to leaders.

Substituting nonviolent resistance for violent responses to tyranny and injustice could create a space for a process to abolish militarism – its structures, hardware and culture. But for nonviolence to constitute an effective remedy for tyranny across the world – including the tyranny of violence itself – it needs to be developed, resourced and applied with as much commitment as we have given to militarism. It needs to become integrated into our curriculum of learning and embedded in our structures – just as militarism is now. While neither war nor nonviolence can provide all-protecting, instant and complete remedies to human wickedness, and although the human condition will always be one of vulnerability, active nonviolence offers us all the opportunity to contribute to each other's safety and wellbeing, while leading us out of the endless cycle of violence. It can enable us to plot a new route to relative security in an ever-shrinking and threatened planet.

The answer to violence lies with all of us. It will not come from the systematic application of more violence, but from a different energy and from the values that reveal violence for what it is. It will come from our waking up to our own place in the scheme of things and deciding to participate in the process of change.

6
Peace, Identity and Participation

*No man is an island, entire of itself; every man is a piece of
the continent, a part of the main; if a clod be washed away by
the sea, Europe is the less, as well as if a promontory were, as
well as if a manor of thy friends or of thine were. Any man's
death diminishes me, because I am involved in mankind.
And therefore never send to know for whom the bell tolls: it
tolls for thee.*

John Donne, *Devotions, no. XVII*

*My brother is dead but I am not looking to atone for his
death. I'm looking to prevent the death of others. The world
is larger than just me. Things don't have to be done to make
up for things that have happened to me. I draw from my love
of human beings that everyone is the same as I am. That it
is possible – not in a dream, but someday – for this to be a
peaceful planet.*

Rita Lasar of New York, who lost her brother in the
World Trade Center attack

*If national boundaries should not be obstacles to trade – we
call it globalization – should they also not be obstacles to
compassion and generosity?*

Howard Zinn, *My Country: The World*

*In 1957 at the Labour Party's debate on disarmament, Aneurin
Bevan declared that he was not prepared to 'go naked into
the conference chamber'… But what was it that Bevan had
to hide? Why should he have been afraid to go naked into
the conference chamber to discuss matters of global life and
death? What he had to hide, as much from himself as from
his adversaries, was nothing less than his humanity.*

Nicholas Humphrey, *An Immodest Proposal*, 1982

All wars are civil wars, because all men are brothers.
Francois Fénelon, bishop and author, 1651–1715

It is in the shelter of each other that the people live.
Irish Proverb

We cannot exist alone, as individuals or as societies. In today's world we are globally interdependent, but our sociability has always been essential to our survival as a species. All our skills – including our ability to think and speak – and our sense of identity, or self, are developed through interaction with others. Our emotional as well as our physical needs are met through our connections with the wider world and those who inhabit it. Our understanding of life and the universe we live in – philosophy, religion and science – represent collective effort. We need each other's help to survive. Even the richest and most powerful of us depend on others for their wellbeing. Modern technology has put us all within reach of each other, so that we – rich and poor alike – must rely on each other's goodwill for our safety. And since we are all reliant on the health of the earth and its ecosystems we depend on each other to co-operate in preserving them.

Yet so much in our current ways of thinking encourages us to forget our interdependence and builds walls between us. In this chapter I want to discuss the very different approach to identity that is necessary to peace: one based on shared humanity and mutual dependence and responsibility. Since the changes I am proposing are profound and difficult, I shall devote the second half of the chapter to the question of how to go about them, looking at a range of challenges, from the practical to the spiritual.

FROM IDENTITY TO IDENTIFICATION[1]

An understanding of identity that is based on difference – between insiders and outsiders, men and women, haves and have-nots – produces fearfulness and disrespect, and overrides compassion. It nurtures, serves and is perpetuated by the culture and structures of domination that give rise to war. Paradoxically, constructions of identity that are focused on difference also involve 'lumping' people together. We identify ourselves (or are identified by others) with a particular generalised group – often extremely diverse and including people we might dislike or disagree with on many issues. We achieve this identification by seeing ourselves as separate from other groups that are probably equally diverse and include many people with whom we would have a great deal in common.

In this approach to identity, our notion of who we *are* is defined in terms of who we are *not*. When the sense of our own identity is weak or under threat we shore it up by sharpening our focus on the otherness of the other, generating enemy images, hostility, fear, and the desire to control, exclude or dominate.[2] On the basis of this notion of separateness, of 'us' and 'them', it is possible for one group or 'nation' to go to war against another. Within this system a collection of people from one country, region or ethnic group can be sent to fight against a collection of people from another, committing acts which would not be possible if they saw each other simply for what they were: as fellow human beings. War involves the violent and wholesale embodiment of prejudice and discrimination. It leaves little or no space for human understanding.

The capacity to identify others *as* other is necessary to our sense of self. But it can be complemented and balanced by a sense of connection and commonality. Our need to strengthen our collective identities by antagonism comes from deep feelings of isolation and alienation – existential and social – but it can be brought into awareness and addressed. Our ways of thinking about ourselves are not the only ways, and they bear no special correspondence to reality. While they may give us solace they also do us harm. Our self-understanding and social attitudes can change, like the cultures they reflect.

Dulce et decorum est pro patria mori – 'It is sweet and fitting to die for one's country'. As the proverb suggests, most wars in recorded history have been fought around the notion of country or nationality. Yet in terms of humanity national identity is a relatively modern idea. Historians and anthropologists tell us that the idea of nationhood came but late upon the scene and that until a few thousand years ago human beings lived in loosely associated family units, with very fluid boundaries.[3]

I have worked with people in many different parts of the world. Even in regions suffering from violent conflict, the majority of those people, when asked about the ways in which they would identify themselves, put 'human beings' first. They acknowledged and celebrated many other diverse categories of belonging – based on family, gender, religion, loves, interests and pursuits. They relished this diversity, yet, by and large, their sense of humanity was overriding.

Where access to television and the internet are common, children growing up now cannot escape awareness of their identity as world citizens, and indeed are embracing it. Vast numbers of human beings find out the hard way (as they have down the centuries) that their existence is not bounded by country – whether through migration forced by war or the necessity of finding work in faraway lands. As a consequence, in many Western cities, new generations of young people are embracing pluralistic, cosmopolitan identities. 'World music' and 'fusion music' are expressions of this sense of global belonging – one that is exciting, not threatening. This is not the crude takeover by one culture of all others but the growth of a counter-culture that celebrates a very broad sense of human identity and embraces diversity as a positive value and enrichment. While the shallow, consumerist fashions of the West have greatly damaged the world's cultural ecosystem, there are also signs that other, long and rich traditions are reasserting themselves.

Young people are also, on average, more aware than their elders of the profound and immediate threats to their environment, and more used to the idea that human beings are but one species among millions, specks in a vast universe. But we are all increasingly aware that not only do we share the same ancestors but we also breathe the same air and are affected by the same global shifts in climate. For all these reasons, and since technology puts us all within each other's reach, to think of humanity as one community (as well as many) seems far from fanciful. I will always remember flying over Europe on a cloudless day, on my way to India, and seeing the land below as a seamless succession of fields and rivers, forests and mountains, with the homely signs of human habitation scattered among them. There were no borders. It was clear that it was the notion of 'a country' that was fanciful. 'My country: the world', seemed the only sensible response.[4]

I recognise that the human community that I am positing is, like nationhood, 'imagined',[5] in that we cannot experience such a wide unit of belonging in day-to-day interaction. There is a different, tangible comradeship that comes with physical presence and doing things together – like living in a family or clan, being part of a football crowd, fighting side by side in an army or marching together for peace. But those particular experiences of community also have their gradations and provide the basis for the idea of a wider, all-human belonging and identification. They give us the experiential information that can help us to hold in our imagination the humanity of strangers and transcend the narrower concepts of identity we have built that cut across our essential recognition of each other: recognition that would quickly be re-established on a desert island.[6]

Because she identifies with other human beings, regardless of other categories, Rita Lasar (quoted at the beginning of this chapter), whose brother was killed in the Twin Towers, wants to save others from a similar fate. In the same way, watching my grandchild suffer intensified my concern for other children and their parents and grandparents. Our particular connections and encounters can support rather than detract from our wider sense of connectedness and interdependence. Empathy is an act of imagination based on our own experience. It is possible because we do share our humanity.

PURPOSES AND VALUES

Whereas in many parts of the world religious affiliation provides a sense of shared identity, in the majority culture of Europe the loss of religious belief, along with political disaffection, has left a gap that is being 'plugged' by consumerism, work and the cult of celebrity and sport. The fading of any real experience of functional social belonging, and the cult of self and self-gratification, have increased the sense of isolation felt by many and robbed us of any sense of purpose. Even families are scattered and family commitments have, by and large, narrowed, weakened and become less permanent. People spend more and more time at work and with work mates – not so much because they are required to, but because their work gives them a sense of who they are. Support for sports teams has reached a degree of intensity that seems explicable only in terms of the identity 'fix' it provides, enhanced by the adversarial nature of the games involved.

Yet, it seems, it is still possible for us to find common cause and a sense of purpose that unites us. In the UK and so many other countries in spring 2003, an unexpected and heartening sense of community was experienced by millions, in response to the threatened war against Iraq. People spent a high proportion of their free time together, thinking and acting with each other, unburdening themselves of pent-up feelings, giving each other moral support and strengthening each other's commitment. Women and men worked together as equals. Their action groups were strikingly non-hierarchical. This was a coming-together not against a common enemy but around shared concerns and values. True, it was a movement *against* war and at times against the politicians pursuing it. But the predominant motivation was one of deep concern, grief and compassion – of moral engagement and a sense of responsibility for people living far away, in another country and culture.

Is it possible that we can find our identity in common values, in a passion for justice, in the impulse of caring for our fellow human beings? Can we focus our desire for control on to problems that confront us all? Can we find excitement and purpose in positive endeavours? I believe that we can, and that nonviolence can offer as great an opportunity for altruism and courage as war ever did.

Anyone who has watched film footage of Gandhi's Salt Marches or the Civil Rights campaign, or the movement to remove President Milosevic from power, can see that there could be nothing more exciting or uniting. Their energy came not from hatred of opponents (not even the Serb campaign against a much reviled leader) but rather from a sense of freedom and common purpose. Similarly, rescue workers freeing people from a mine or a collapsed building will experience a drive for achievement that is wholly positive. We have all, at some time in our lives, felt and witnessed the kind of energy that comes from a shared human purpose.

We cannot fail to be aware that in some contexts the renewal of identity is being achieved not by common endeavour in pursuit of humane values but through a retreat into harsh versions of old cultural patterns, involving the rejection of what, in terms of care and respect, have been advances – such as the liberation of women. But in other circumstances communities and societies have combined new norms and understandings with valuable old traditions – for instance, those of community, hospitality and care for the weak.

Although it has to be admitted that religious allegiance, like clan loyalty, is often boosted by hostility, the idea of a common human identity is fundamental to all world religions. Societies of belief, like other social units, can – and often do – function in caring, co-operative and altruistic ways. That is not surprising since, according to biologists and anthropologists, these tendencies are built into our genes.[7] They are our measure of our own dignity and self-respect. They underlie the very concept of humanity.

We *need* to belong, and in order to hold together, communities and individuals alike need a sense of purpose – whether mundane or dramatic, personal or political. The causes that draw people together can be about working *for* something as well as against. If our concern is each other's wellbeing, there is no shortage of such causes. Even without the help of war and greed, calamity can strike any of us at any time. The most fortunate individuals and societies experience times when they need the support of others. And there are plenty of common threats to unite us, from climate change to meteorites. There are also all sorts of positive endeavours that will be more successful when we pool our efforts – from having fun to developing knowledge, from exploring the universe to coping with infirmity.

Instead of fighting against the realities of our fragility and mortality, and against each other as a proxy for them, we need to come to terms with them. Instead of trying to inure ourselves against life and the dying that is part of it, we need to go with it, if not embrace it. Whatever our beliefs or non-beliefs, we can find our immortality in the wider reality of which we are part. Thinking in this way could help us to loosen our stranglehold on life and on each other, to live creatively rather than destructively.[8]

The values of care and responsibility for others (stereotypically associated with femininity) can give us a non-antagonistic sense of purpose and draw on the humanity of men and women alike. They can embrace both domestic and international policy and action. They can enable us to build co-operative power with others to improve each other's lives.

One great problem with pluralist approaches and universalist values is that they threaten more closed belief systems and appear to set themselves up as superior to them – just a particular form of

Enlightenment colonialism. The resurgence of conservative forms of religion is a response not only to growing moral aimlessness but also to insensitive and arrogant assumptions that 'modern' is best and that Western mores should be imposed on others in a globalisation of culture. Yet I want to suggest that there can be universally agreed values that offer a global solution.

How can we square this circle? Firstly, I think, by a common recognition of the plight we are in – that in our various ways and cultures we have failed in human decency and respect and have a long way to go if we are to start measuring up to any of our ideals. Secondly, we need to hold on firmly and passionately to certain values, yet to do so with modesty and respect, recognising that we are also a product of many influences – and that we fall short of our own ideals. If we are open to learning, our thinking will, in turn, be challenged and changed by what others have to say to us. Combining the very different energies of commitment and diffidence means developing our powers of balance, but it can only be done if our respect for ourselves and for others is genuine.

The fundamental value of unconditional care and respect for all human beings is too important to be hidden or apologised for, though its application and inherent dilemmas need to be a matter for ongoing reflection, exchange and debate, drawing on the insights and experiences of all cultures. To promote it is not to corrupt the world with crude, anything-goes arrogance but to insist on the dignity of people, to stand up for humanity. And the more we encompass all beings in our respect and care, the more humane we shall become.

We have to get beyond the either–or debate about individual identity and choice on the one hand, and community and culture on the other. They are part of each other, constantly interacting. In her brilliant, personal account of moving from one culture to another, Eva Hoffman refers to the 'unassimilable' part of herself and of all of us that we need to find if we are to 'know that we exist not only within culture but also outside it'.[9] The bedrock of our collective moral resources is personal conscience and responsibility. We cannot use culture to escape from it.

PARTICIPATION[10]

Whether by action or inaction, we are in fact bound to influence each other's lives since, in John Donne's words, we are 'involved in mankind'. Honouring our interdependence implies participation in the business of society, on the basis of human equality. This we can do directly, by caring for one another in living communities, giving service to them, supporting and participating in collective activities for the common good (including enjoyment). Participation of this kind will involve both collective decision-making and collective or delegated action. At the community level, these things can happen informally.

When it comes to larger units, the notion of politics comes into play, with its baggage of collective ideologies associated with political parties. Perhaps if we could agree to rethink our ways of managing public affairs we might be able to find a very different model, but the basic idea of democracy seems good: 'Government by the people; that form of government in which the sovereign power resides in the people as a whole, and is exercised by them … or by officers elected by them.'[11] In our current reality, however, the idea of the sovereign power residing in the people seems a remote dream. In the UK, certainly, democracy for most people means nothing beyond turning out to vote occasionally, and the proportion of people who do even that is decreasing all the time. I believe this alienation from public affairs both results from and contributes to the sense of purposelessness that afflicts us.

If non-participation doesn't make us happy, neither does it further our real interests. Wars are fought largely for the benefit of leaders and elites, whether political or financial, and their costs are borne largely by ordinary people. That is an indication that democracy as we now practise it (or rather fail to practise it) is not working for our good or for the good of others.

Wars are fought in our name, with our money and, in as far as they are needed, our young people. We become prey to the ambitions of leaders whose interests are not ours. To live in a world of war and terror cannot be for the general good – yet we allow it to happen. Economies are run in ways that enrich the already wealthy and do not uplift the poor. Yet the local and international economic mechanisms that adversely affect the lives of millions are made by politicians put in place by our (collective) vote or non-vote. To make matters worse, we have allowed a great deal of the power which was in theory exercised on our behalf to be handed over to big businesses that exploit the world's people and resources for their own ends. As individuals who purchase what those businesses produce, we then compound our passivity with active collusion.

The fable writer, Aesop, told a tale of frogs living in a particular pond, who wished to avoid the effort of ordering their own society and petitioned Jupiter to send them a king to do it for them. He sent them a log, which by the splash it made induced sufficient terror in them to hold sway in their pond for a while. Eventually, however, realising that their ruler was a sham, they asked for a replacement, whereupon the god sent them a stork, which immediately consumed them. Though the secondary moral of the story was that the monarch you knew was to be preferred to the one you did not, the fable's primary lesson was that those who had any self-respect and good sense would choose to manage their own affairs.

This is an apt and salutary tale for the twenty-first century. Those of us who live in relatively comfortable societies with apparently innocuous governments have been bought off by temporary, local prosperity and have chosen, by and large, to abdicate our own responsibilities for justice and for peace. Predatory leaders have been allowed to take power, in 'traditional' and 'modern' societies alike. Even those who seemed less predatory and more socially responsible have in turn abdicated power to 'market forces' and colluded with them, giving us the benefit of log–predator power sharing.

Care and responsibility for others, and for common needs and purposes, implies participation in affairs beyond our own domestic ones. And here, I believe, lies the problem. When our own wellbeing is not immediately threatened, we tend to succumb to indolence. It is laziness, rather than enmity, that is the greatest obstacle to practical caring. If our connections with those who bear the brunt of 'power-over' policies were clearer and more immediate and if the necessity of our participation for the survival of democracy was more apparent to us, we might find the energy to act. But we have become acclimatised to isolated indolence and for most of us our only association with collective endeavours is as consumers. Just as remoteness weakens our moral resources and makes the violence of war possible, so it makes the will for public responsibility and action hard to generate. We make efforts for those near and dear to us, but it takes more to elicit a response from us when those needing our care are far away. And it is hard to see ourselves as necessary participants when the machinery of public life is invisible to us.

If we want government of the people by the people and for the people, and if we want to forge societies that would be capable of non-military defence against tyranny, we shall have to overcome our laziness. We shall have to give up some of the hours spent watching other people's lives – real and imaginary – on television, and spend more time living our own. We shall have to channel more of our sociability into working together to shape our lives and less into standing around with glasses or beer mugs in our hands. We shall have to apply our brains to the philosophical and practical conundrums associated with trying to balance autonomy with social responsibility and the benefits of scale, achieved by working within large units, with the need to devolve power and responsibility to the local level. If we are to engage each other in the common business that affects us, we need to do so as far as possible in contexts where human beings can interact directly. If we are to find ways of making human nature work for all human beings, not just the few, we need that human encounter that releases our moral resources instead of blocking or dissipating them, as remoteness does.

There has probably never been a genuine and complete *direct* democracy anywhere, ever: a society in which every member was involved in the decision-making and participated in seeing that agreed policies were carried out. Even our efforts at representative democracy leave many of us unrepresented and put us at such a distance from power and responsibility that we feel cynical and disengaged.

It is hard to imagine a significantly different system. It would presuppose a degree of willingness to experiment, take risks and commit time that would be quite foreign to us. But if we want to get away from the politics of domination to the politics of co-operation, I believe we need to do far better than we have ever done so far. We shall probably never achieve full participation – whatever that would mean or look like. But we do need to achieve a substantial shift away from supine dependency on a few power-holders to a situation in which a substantial proportion of the population feels involved in and responsible for influencing political policy and decisions.

If our way of doing politics is to reflect our human equality and interdependence and contribute to our general wellbeing, and in particular to move us away from war, then it will be based not on antagonism and the power to get the better of others but on service and the widest possible co-operation. I do not mean to suggest that there should be no differences and no debate; only that the wellbeing of people should be the centre point, not the success of one political party or another. And that where there is a substantial degree of consensus, so that it is feasible for different actors to work together for the common good, they should do so. If the party system is to remain, it should do so in a humbler, less ambitious and more democratic version. But maybe we can come up with something better.

ACHIEVING CHANGE

I am suggesting that if we are to move beyond war, violence and injustice, fundamental change is needed in our understanding of our own identity and in our attitude to collective responsibility. How can this be brought about? To commit oneself to action to bring about change, one must first be aware and convinced of its necessity. Since most people are not yet aware or convinced, and therefore not about to act, those of us who are must get on with the business of convincing others.

There are days when I feel such changes are impossible – that those who see their necessity will always remain a small minority. But then I remember that, according to the laws of inertia, although it is very hard to get things moving, once the process starts, increasingly they gather their own momentum. And I think of geometric progression and see that even large changes can take place in a short time. A review of life in the twentieth century will show how quickly things can be transformed – for good and ill. With technological advance has come a great acceleration in the pace of social change. And just as technological development can be a resource for solving problems rather than creating them, for nurturing life rather than destroying it, so the mutability of cultures opens up the possibility of positive transformation, as well as dissolution or degradation. A time of crisis is not only fraught with danger, it is also a moment of opportunity. Remember the millions across the world who demonstrated – many of them for the first time in their lives – against the war on Iraq. They showed that mobilisation was possible.

Here I want to revert to the theory that culture, action and structures constitute a triangle of elements that create, reinforce and change each other, so that working on one corner of the triangle has an impact also on the others. And I want to combine this theory with the idea that change needs to take place on three levels: personal, social and political. If we can start changing things on all corners of the triangle and at all three levels, we can expect the process to take on its own cumulative dynamic.

The first thing we need to do is to wake up, to become aware[12] of the issues that confront us. Then, having woken up to our situation and responsibilities, we must start thinking for ourselves rather than simply accepting – or ignoring – what we are told. We must start re-examining our own assumptions, attitudes and values; relating them to our own behaviour and to what is going on around us; exploring our assumptions about relationships; challenging our 'banal nationalism'.[13]

The most radical change needed in relation to public affairs is a general awakening of responsibility and a consequent will to act – on whatever issue and at whatever level: from ringing up the local Highways Department to report a broken traffic light to joining in public discussion about local health care; from lobbying Parliament about international trade legislation to blockading the entrance to a nuclear base; from joining the school governors to being on an adoption panel; from protest to advocacy to service.

In societies where life for the majority is relatively comfortable, the biggest obstacle to overcome will be inertia rather than fear. The greatest need will be for effort rather than courage. I remember one US activist who went round Britain in the 1960s speaking on the theme of 'afflicting the comfortable'.[14] Those of us who have been too comfortable for too long do need to be afflicted, but we also need to lose our cynicism and to be encouraged to see that we can do something for good. We need to be allowed to think, to start with at least, that to do something is better than to do nothing. We need relatively unthreatening entry points into what, for many of us, will be new lives as activists. If we make the threshold too high we shall be left with another form of elitism. We need the participation of the many even more than the heroism of the few. As one colleague recently put it, the first vital step is simply to 'show up'.

Advocates of nonviolence often argue that its power comes from the willingness of its adherents to act heroically and suffer harsh consequences – just as in war soldiers, trained to kill, may be required to die.[15] People who choose to risk their lives to confront tyranny, or who devote all their energy to challenging the disastrous iniquities of the current capitalist-militarist system, deserve our thanks and admiration. Their role is vital. But it is wasted without the smaller courage and humbler efforts of the many, and it is this more 'ordinary' need that poses the greatest challenge.

If the movement for change is to practise the inclusiveness that it is promoting, it must welcome people who have no habits of engagement, or whose energies are low, or whose lives are so packed with other necessary commitments that their available time is small and the risks they can take are minimal. It must not appear that there is no room for those who offer quiet support in small ways. In practice engagement breeds more engagement. Signing a petition may be a step towards writing a letter or attending a meeting – and bringing a friend. That in turn may encourage participation in the next demonstration or joining the planning group – so long as there is encouragement rather than pressure, and opportunities of all kinds to become involved.

Until recently, the peace movement has been an ageing one. That seems to be changing and we need to make sure that it does change. While it is quite unacceptable for those of us who have participated in the system that has produced the current mess to wash our hands of it, we need the ideas, leadership and energy of young people. It will be interesting to see whether they are expressed through their own, new initiatives or by swelling the ranks of existing organisations and transforming them.

Active participation may require alterations to our relationships, life patterns and priorities, so that we spend less time making money and consuming, and more time on living out our social responsibilities. But once we have developed the habits of awareness, such changes will seem right and necessary. They will bring their own rewards, in terms of a greater sense of integrity, purpose and involvement – of acting more constructively and filling out a missing dimension of our lives.

There are vital contributions that can be made by individuals, whether from home or in their workplace: thinking, writing and speaking, generating new ideas, shifting opinions and influencing policy. All of us can play a role at some level through such activities – talking to friends, writing letters to newspapers and MPs, raising issues with professional bodies and so on. Individual action is important and for some of us this will constitute our most effective contribution. For others it will be the only one that is possible.

But there are things that can be achieved collectively that cannot be done in another context or alone. Local groups play a key role in movement building, enabling individuals to support and encourage each other and engage in collective action. They are microcosms of society, providing us with the opportunity to put into practice the values that motivate us – and to discover just how difficult that can be! But if we really are to bring about change, we need to put into practice the ideas we are seeking to promote and embody our values in our action. If we want to work for a participatory society, that should be reflected in the way we work together. If one of our core values is respect, we should respect each other. The encouragement and active involvement of all the group's membership will also maximise its power for change. The role of leadership within the group should therefore be to enable all to participate to maximum effect, rather than to act for the group or dictate to it.

Forming a group and establishing trust requires time and attention, but the effort will be well rewarded in terms of both effectiveness and enjoyment. Getting the job done and sustaining energy and commitment are mutually dependent aspects of group life. Doing things well and achieving what we set out to do is not only important in itself but will be good for morale and encourage people to stay involved. Equally, well-run meetings, that are interesting and fun as well as hard work, will help us to be effective. When we come to regard fellow-members as special friends we find it easier to stay committed.

Building and sustaining effective groups involves:

- Shared values and goals; agreement over methods as well as purposes; honesty about differences; trust.
- Clear roles and the distribution of power and responsibility.
- Agreement about systems and processes which are transparent and participatory.
- Regular meetings – reporting back, reflecting, developing new plans.
- Careful preparation and facilitation of meetings (with training if necessary).
- An understanding that having fun together is important, as well as getting the work done, and that good strategies call for both analysis and imagination.
- Openness to newcomers, and willingness to draw them in and give them responsibility, 'capitalising' on all the skills available.
- Appreciating each other's strengths and tolerating each other's weaknesses.
- Dealing with conflicts openly and constructively.
- Understanding each other's circumstances and accepting each other's choices – no 'guilt trips'.
- Thorough analysis, clear goals and careful planning.
- Regular evaluation, both of work done and of group process, for the recognition of achievement and for greater effectiveness.

The problems that need to be addressed are so many and so huge that it is easy for the most committed individuals and groups to feel paralysed. No one can do everything but we can all do something. We can give minimal (perhaps financial) support to some things and put our main effort into one particular aspect of the broad movement for peace, justice and (real) democracy – an inseparable trio of interdependent movements. It is important to be aware of their inter-relatedness. But although making groups work well is difficult, it is at least a limited task with a clear focus. Building sustainable coalitions of different organisations and groups, let alone broad movements and coalitions of movements, is infinitely more difficult.

I dream of a coherent, concerted, effective global alliance between environmentalists, people working for economic justice, human rights campaigners of all kinds, feminists, and the peace movement. In terms of organisation I am sceptical. The units of which a movement is made up are myriad, differing in size, in membership, in style, even in values. There is and could be no unifying structure. Even coalitions with a limited focus are difficult to achieve and sustain, with their competing tendencies and belief-systems: Marxists vying with anarchists, liberals with radicals, utopians with those who see themselves as realists. Moreover, participants in movements come and go. Enthusiasms wane, life circumstances change, the faithful grow old and die, and new people come in. And just as movements fluctuate and change from within, so they are also affected by changes in the world around them.

How is it possible, then, for us ever to be concerted enough to effect the changes we want to see? I think we must concentrate on building coherence at the level of understanding and orientation, enlarging our own thinking, opening our minds to what we can learn from the perceptions of people who share some, at least, of our values, but see the world from different perspectives. We must find ways of affirming and building common core values and understand we are all part of a movement that is wider than our own particular vision can encompass, though we will keep enlarging our capacity to see.

Fortunately perhaps, change too is unpredictable and, on the big scale, beyond managing. It comes about in unexpected ways and at unexpected times. Past 'failures' prepare the ground for later success. Apparently independent, even random, events can catalyse or create a synergy with our messy, chaotic and fluctuating movements – boost failing energies, give new focus to dissipated attention and bring about an explosion of activity, opening the way for unexpected progress and more radical transformation.

In the meantime, we can only work away at the things we have identified as our own priorities, matching our knowledge and skills, concerns and passions to the vast range of what is needed. We can get together with others who have chosen the same focus, joining or forming local groups to work as consistently and effectively as we can. We can make our own contribution, but be aware of the wider movement and the different groups and networks that are part of it. We can work for the different levels of change that are needed – personal change, educating and developing ourselves, changing our lifestyles; social change, educating others and engaging in dialogue with them (which will also change us); political change, engaging and influencing those whose job it is to represent us and those who make political decisions.

Improving our own skills as thinkers, communicators and organisers is vital to our effectiveness. If our object is to win others over to our point of view, to enable them to see what we see, we need to be good listeners as well as articulate advocates. It will assist our cause, as well as honour our values, if we seek common ground with those who oppose us, as well as naming clearly the things we want to change. It is vital that we regard even our toughest adversaries as capable of learning and shifting and that we avoid the self-indulgence of belittling others by the way we speak and write. We are so used to the dynamics of battle that the practice of constructive dialogue can seem strange and inadequate.

We must not dig a new pit for ourselves by believing in an 'us' that is all good and a 'them' that is all bad. None of us can claim total fidelity to our highest values. We all contribute, in one way or another, to humanity's problems and none of us has all the answers to the dilemmas inherent in the human condition. But we can choose to put our best efforts into finding the best ways possible for living with each other. We can work on the assumption that we, like others, have the capacity for good and the potential for growth and healing, as individuals and as societies. Humility and self-respect are not incompatible. We need both if we are to learn to respect others. If we accept our own fallibility, we may get better at accepting that people who are different from us – even those who currently think and do things we know are bad – may also have good qualities and potential.

The most fundamental motivation for long-term activism – participation in society as a regular part of one's life – is a sense of identity that includes moral agency. This is what keeps activists going. It is part of their understanding of who they are, how they see themselves in the world – as part of a web of mutual responsibility. Whether or not this understanding is set in a wider religious or philosophical framework, it is the bedrock of their lives – the reason they get up in the morning. To ignore it would be to undermine their own wellbeing.

Though this way of thinking and being might seem to be confined to relatively few people, altruism, the capacity to act with other people's good in mind, if necessary at the expense of one's own, is integral to human nature. Even 'bad' people will rise to it in some circumstances. We have to think beyond ourselves to sustain ourselves psychologically.

For many of us, the past century swept away old certainties, bringing new freedoms but with them a kind of loneliness or emptiness that made the human condition in many ways harder to live with and led to a profound existential unease. For others it seemed as if all that they stood for and valued was scorned and threatened by modernity and post-modernity. Liberal forms of religion seemed inadequate to withstand the assault, and the certainties of fundamentalism offered a stronger fortress.

Human beings have always, it seems, constructed belief systems for themselves. Often those belief systems have had a malign effect. They have motivated, or been used to justify, violence and cruelty: human sacrifices, 'holy' wars, torture and burning, pogroms and gulags. Yet if we ignore the human need to construct frameworks of understanding for their lives, relating to the wider reality of which they are part, we shall not be able to work *with* that need and draw on it as source for good rather than allowing it to magnify our worst tendencies. What is essential is that our understanding of who we are and what we should be doing has a moral basis; that humane values are at its heart.

Whatever the circumstances in which we live, we cannot be absolved of responsibility for our cultures or our belief systems, whether given or chosen. Our moral capacity obliges us to evaluate them. We do need them. At their best they can contribute to our internal wellbeing and social empowerment. But, even if we believe they (or we) are inspired, they are formulated, interpreted and constantly re-made by us. Whether we call it super-ego, soul or spirit, we all have a part or aspect of ourselves that is touched by the transcendent, that measures things by a yardstick not related to self-gratification but profoundly embedded in our deepest sense of self, that values what it recognises as good. We need to nurture that capacity, not ignore it.

And we urgently need the widest possible global conversation about the values and inspiration that can draw us together as human beings and provide us with a basis for the coexistence and co-operation we so desperately need. We all have a responsibility to help make that conversation happen.[16]

7
Time for Action

The term 'national security' has a built-in contradiction. In the atomic age no national security is possible. Either we have a workable world security system or we have nothing.

Norman Cousins

War is as outmoded as cannibalism, chattel slavery, blood feuds and duelling – an insult to God and humanity.

Muriel Lester

Never before in the history of the world has there been a global, visible, public, viable, open dialogue and conversation about the very legitimacy of war.

Dr Robert Muller, former assistant secretary general of the United Nations, now Chancellor emeritus of the University of Peace in Costa Rica

The corporate revolution will collapse if we refuse to buy what they are selling – their ideas, their version of history, their wars, their weapons, their notion of inevitability. Remember this: We be many and they be few. They need us more than we need them ... Another world is not only possible, she is on her way. On a quiet day, I can hear her breathing.

Arundhati Roy, *Confronting Empire*

Together, let us reject the clamour of fear and listen to the whisperings of hope.

Aotearoa/New Zealand Quakers

I think that people want peace so much that one of these days government had better get out of the way and let them have it.

President Eisenhower

The world we live in is in many ways both baffling and depressing. If we care, we often feel powerless. Yet we cannot deny our capacity and duty to act to prevent and address what is wrong, even if we don't yet know the answer. Despair is a luxury we cannot afford. Life is full of dilemmas and yet we have to pick our way through them. And if we think about our collective resources, rather than our collective problems, we can see that change – even radical change – is indeed possible. But we need to be clear what is at stake.

WHAT NEEDS TO BE DONE AND WHY

The situation in which we find ourselves, as a species, is violent and globally insecure. Our current, dominatory approach to coexistence is dysfunctional. War, a manifestation of the culture and structures of domination, cannot be a solution to their destructive dynamics. Each time an individual war is fought, the system of war is perpetuated and entrenched, along with all that it represents and involves. It consumes and destroys resources to equally obscene degrees and inflicts unimaginable suffering on those caught up in it. Most wars are fought for reasons that are at best mixed and are related more to the interests of the few than the needs of the many. Their impact on the lives of ordinary people is disastrous.

War can topple regimes but it cannot make peace, being a contradiction of its values and ethics, which demand mutual respect and the wholehearted acknowledgement of human equality, rights and responsibilities. Any war is a crime against humanity.[1] Yet the myth of war's inevitability and effectiveness has provided a context in which elites have pursued their own agendas with relatively little challenge. While the argument of 'last resort' is often used, it is seldom – if ever – justified, since leaders' attempts to find alternatives are more often than not derisory. There *are* alternatives to war as a means of addressing violence and injustice – achieving just ends. The power of the few cannot be maintained without the acquiescence of the many. The last century saw not only a terrible number of cruel wars but also some staggering examples of the effectiveness of nonviolent civilian action. It overthrew tyrants and changed the face of international relations. Yet such is the strength of the myth of war and the old beliefs in militarism that we have scarcely digested that reality.

Although human beings have undoubted capacities for aggression and cruelty, they are not doomed to continue killing each other and squandering their resources in elaborate systems for doing so. Inter-group violence is a relatively recent phenomenon in the history of humanity. Though for the last few thousand years we have developed hierarchical systems and cultures that sanction and glorify violence, that is not the best of which we are capable. Though we may be influenced and shaped by our context, we also have the power to change it.

If we are to relegate war to the history books – as we can and must – we will need to draw on and develop the constructive means of addressing conflict that are commonplace in all our cultures but are all too rarely tried and never exhausted in international relations. We must take nonviolent methods as seriously – and if necessary fund them as generously – as we currently do our military methods (though since nonviolence destroys nothing and requires no hardware, its costs can never be so great). We must develop the attitudes, skills and capacities necessary for preventing violence and resolving conflict, and the methods of civil resistance and intervention for situations where conflict prevention and resolution have failed and violence is ongoing. We must support and harness the goodwill and energy of ordinary people in acting for change and building genuine peace. We must think globally and act locally. Putting our own house in order will have a huge impact on the possibilities of making others' more habitable.

If the rich nations put half of the effort into justice that they currently put into defending vested interests; if they stopped talking about the 'debts' of others and started to seek forgiveness and make reparation for their own indebtedness; if they would start working for fair trade agreements rather than exploitative ones; if they began behaving democratically in world forums rather than trying to force other countries to line up with them through bribing and bullying, relationships would be transformed and the world would rapidly become more secure for both the haves and have-nots. If 'modern' societies were more self-critical and recognised that they had something to learn from, as well as something to offer to others, their ideas might be taken more seriously. If the big powers applied the approaches and procedures of conflict resolution to their own relationships with others, the face of international politics would be transformed.

Nothing can alter our vulnerability as human beings, or our capacity to harm each other. But we will do better if our norms, behaviour and systems are focused on looking after rather than attacking and undermining each other. Since we are interdependent, common security is our best bet. We are specks in a vast universe,[2] prey to all manner of forces beyond our control. To cope with the adversities of life and increase its benefits, to minimise suffering and maximise joy, we shall do far better with co-operation than with antagonism. To consume ourselves in mutual hostility is pathetically foolish, but it is not our only option.

If we really try to do this – recognise that we can choose and abolish war – there will be moral dilemmas to face. Moving from one paradigm to another will be no easy thing. Will we really be able to manage the violence imbedded in the old system when the new one is not yet in place? How will we deal with those who hang on to their weapons when the rest of us have handed them in (metaphorically and literally)? I have done my best to address these issues, which already confront us. They are part of the whole challenge of dealing with violence nonviolently, which will always remain, to some degree, and will continue to be acute so long as current relationships and structures are in place. And yet, for that very reason, we have to make that transition.

It is hard even to *imagine* ourselves out of one paradigm and into another – let alone set about making that transfer a reality – and the transition is fraught with dilemmas of every kind. How can we extricate ourselves from the mire of our current situation without constantly being sucked back into it? How can we step out of the cycle of violence, squaring the demands of justice with the needs of peace?

There will be times when it is hard to resist the 'need' for war when war really does seem to be the least bad option. We need to start preparing – on a realistic scale, with proper resources – for constructive solidarity and intervention, so that we are not left as bystanders while atrocities happen. But if atrocities are ever to stop happening we need to bring the juggernaut of war to a halt.

In the past, nonviolent societies have been overwhelmed by violent ones. We have to make sure that we are sufficiently prepared to ensure that that cannot happen again. We have many resources for dealing with violence constructively, but there will be major risks and difficulties. My argument is that we have to make the break somehow and that since this is a necessary task the moral responsibility for managing the dilemmas inherent in it should be shared by all and not left at the door of what is now seen as the pacifist fringe. We should all own the agenda and share the task, wrestling with the problems, contributing our ideas and adding our commitment, recognising that the transition needs to be made. If the changes we initiate are global rather than piecemeal, that in itself will make for greater security.

We cannot see the future or know the distant outcomes of our actions, but we can work for a better understanding of our nature and of our place in the universe. We have so much in common that our differences are minute by comparison. And one thing we all have in common, whatever our belief system and culture, is our failure to follow through with any consistency on our most humane values. We can promote these values in our societies and change our cultures for the better. We can choose to foster our ability to care for each other, to enjoy each other and to build satisfying and life-enhancing relationships and communities. We can develop new forms of participatory democracy and new models for economic exchange and co-operation. We can establish practices and structures – social, political and economic – that serve the needs of all of us, our 'common wealth', and protect all members of society.

I am not a utopian – unless that means simply wanting the best that we can manage. I believe we will all, always, have to wrestle with our insecurities and destructive tendencies, resist the temptation to boost our individual and collective egos by despising or bettering someone else. But I also believe we can foster our strengths and constructive capacities, personally, socially and politically. We can learn to deal with our inevitable conflicts constructively and to make that the norm for international as well as social and domestic life. After all, we do mostly manage to get along with each other without killing those we disagree with or blowing up the houses or offices of those who seem to threaten us in some way. We think that is 'normal', and so it should be.

Strengthening and developing a peace culture will involve marrying the 'masculine' concepts of strength and heroism with the 'female' values of care and nurture. We can develop identities based on empathy and identification rather than perceptions of difference and rivalry. We shall also need to rediscover the value of community at the local and global level. Such a re-visioning of relationships implies a radical rethink of units and structures of governance. The relatively recent and already evolving notion of the state as the primary unit of political organisation needs to be deconstructed and, at the very least, modified.

At present many people are resisting the transfer of powers from states to larger conglomerates and their fears are understandable. But the direction of change need not be towards ever-greater control by larger and larger units. It can be towards the empowerment of local people and structures, within a global framework: one designed to protect the freedom and equality of all people, based on the notion of common security and common wealth. Nationalism is built on the substitution of 'imagined communities' for real ones. The expansion of global awareness and community action will be the best answer to it. Our first community must be a community of values rather than of political units.

Working on such a broad agenda is, to say the least, difficult. Militarism will be much harder to overcome than any dictatorship. Its power is more insidious and its tentacles reach into every sphere of human organisation, as well as into our very language and thinking. (Try noting the number of times in a day that you use a military metaphor.) The many and powerful vested interests will be hard to overcome and the dynamics of our current systems have their own huge inertia. It is impossible to delineate the steps in the many and intertwining paths in the broad route from here to there, or predict the dynamics that will be created by changes in one sphere impacting on another. Moral dilemmas will continue to confront us all as we struggle to move forward. There is not much ground for confidence and no room at all for arrogance, but the attempt must be made. War is like an addiction. It is in our system and there will never be a good time to give it up.

GETTING ON WITH THE JOB

The present moment is one of great threat and widespread misery. At the same time it is a moment of great opportunity. Never before has there been such a worldwide movement against military action. Unfortunately, it is not yet a movement against war as such, but it opens questions pointing in that direction. Until now the peace movement has failed to sustain itself, waking and growing only when a particular war was threatened. We must change that, using opposition to particular wars as the way in to generating a more general and fundamental debate and a re-evaluation of war itself.

Building a mass constituency for the abolition of war will involve passionate and informed advocacy. It will also involve open dialogue between people who see the world from very different perspectives. If we are to make the transition from domination to co-operation, we must work together towards the same end. Since the way ahead will be complex and difficult, we must learn, on all sides, to live with and acknowledge uncertainty as well as conviction, find our way forward with determination, sure of our values and direction. Rigid ideological and religious frameworks must give way to a vibrant and profound commitment to humanity itself and all that is good in it, nurtured by a diversity of cultural and inspirational frameworks and communities. Above all, loyalty to values must override loyalty to group or state.

Learning needs to take place within the movement as well as beyond it. I have many good colleagues who oppose 'capitalist' wars but not 'revolutionary' ones. They think that those who oppose all wars don't take structural injustice seriously. We must show that we do, and that war and injustice are inextricably linked. We also need to persuade the 'peace starts in our hearts' people that politics matter, and those who have no time for personal transformation that changing ourselves is part of changing society.

I hope we will recognise that we have more things in common than things dividing us and that all of us have a role to play; that our differences allow us to fulfil different roles and reach out to different constituencies. At the local level we seem able to be more relaxed about the variety of our viewpoints, to build trust in spite of them and even to modify our views through engaging with each other's ideas. We need to tell our organisations that we want co-operation rather than warfare. If we are to transform the structures and interests that make for war, we are going to have to use every ounce of our energy constructively.

We must work to make decency and kindness the hallmarks of our movement – not only in terms of our aspirations but in the way we think and act. While it is vital – life-giving – to oppose what is cruel and destructive (which is why I have spent more than half this book arguing the case for war's abolition) it is also essential that we project a positive message that embodies our visions for human society; that we run on hope and goodwill as well as anger; that we do not fall into the trap of demonising people but work to win friends; that we remember that the way we act now will help shape the future we are working for.

As I have suggested, we may need to change our lifestyles if we are to have the time and energy to become more effective. We need to pay as much attention to the quality of our campaigning as we do to our professional work. That will require something of a culture change. We must not sacrifice friendliness and enthusiasm to efficiency, but building our effectiveness will make our efforts not only more productive but more rewarding.

Here are some examples of the work to be undertaken.[3] The list is long and doubtless could be longer:

1. Expose the destructiveness and cruelty of militarism and of current approaches to power, and the influence of vested interests, through education and debate at all levels and in many different circles – political, academic, professional, popular (movements) and artistic.
2. Expose the myth of war's necessity and efficacy, and its cultural roots in destructive models of masculinity and power.
3. Promote debate at all levels about the purposes of 'foreign policy' and international relations.
4. Support conscientious objectors to armed service and to paying taxes to fund wars.
5. Expand direct resistance to military activities.
6. Challenge war in the courts (local and international).
7. Campaign for an end to the arms trade.
8. Call for a ban on the private armies of big businesses.
9. Make known past and present covert involvement in conflicts authorised by governments.
10. Campaign for an end to the arms race and for global disarmament, promoting international policies based on the notion of common security.

11. Identify and draw into the movement those who have been seen as 'on the other side' – in particular, politicians and retired or disaffected members of the military (there are plenty out there).
12. Embark on a programme of popular education on war and its impact and the needs of peace.
13. Make known the philosophy, strategies and successes of nonviolence, as an alternative to war in dealing with injustice and oppression, and the concepts and practice of conflict resolution as a way of addressing differences.
14. Press for new research on civilian defence and a programme to make it feasible.
15. Train ourselves and our children as communicators and actors, visionaries and strategists, philosophers and politicians and act to transform relationships and build peace in our own communities.
16. Use good conflict transformation practice to handle conflicts at the local level.
17. Support and promote government funding for 'conflict prevention' initiatives and their elevation in importance above military spending and activity. Challenge the logic and morality of militarism in relation to these constructive approaches. Promote policies based on the notion of 'common security' and sufficiency.
18. Encourage new forms of history, writing about the past and present from the point of view of those who have seemed to have no power, so that we recognise that we are all part of history and its making.
19. Promote debate about identity, including gender, ethnicity, religion, promoting the idea of 'moral identity'[4] and universal values; seek to build a community of values that transcends specific religions, ideologies and cultures.
20. Promote new models of masculinity and femininity and a new, liberating approach to gender.
21. Demand and build women's involvement in politics and in peacebuilding at every level.
22. Include children in public debate and participation.
23. Support the campaign for the reform of international economic institutions and regulations, and for economic redistribution, making the link between economic justice,

simpler lifestyles and the abolition of militarism as the arbiter of power.

24. Forge North–South alliances wherever possible; make links with, learn from and support the newly emerging non-aligned movement.

25. Promote thinking on economic rights as human rights.

26. Make links with those concerned for ethics in business.

27. Support and work with the environmentalist movement, pointing to the disastrous ecological consequences of war and relating respect for the earth with respect for each other and the concept of coexistence.

28. Support and work with the human rights movement, exposing war as an organised, mass form of human rights abuse.

29. Build solidarity networks – local and global – between peace activists and those focusing on economic justice, human rights and environmental protection.

30. Promote and engage in active solidarity with local activists in all those spheres.

31. Support movements for political reform – including party democracy and moving away from the antagonistic, bi-polar model and towards pluralism, honesty and open debate. Be tenacious in holding politicians accountable for what is done in our name, vociferous in supporting good measures and in challenging bad ones.

32. Engage directly in party politics to work for change from within the system.

33. Expose the current corruption and manipulation of the United Nations and support the global movement for its reform and strengthening.

34. Build connections with the mass communication media (which can be useful and even supportive despite their manipulation by owners and governments) and hold them to account. Use correspondence channels to foster conversation about values, beliefs and the future, from both local and international perspectives.

35. Act as an alternative source of public information through public meetings, news-sheets and websites.

36. Connect with local organisations and authorities, making the links between international and local manifestations

of violence and injustice and working for the local implementation of policies that support global justice and demilitarisation. Help raise the profile of different forms of local participation.

37. Encourage academic contributions to all the above.
38. Use every means to awaken people's sense of power, responsibility and connectedness, as an antidote to alienation. Help them to see that if we all participate things can change. Indeed, they will have changed.

As I say, the list is long and could be longer. No one of us can work on everything but we can all work on something. Some will be heroic in the time they give, others in the nature of their action. The rest of us will make more modest contributions. We shall succeed if we can build, sustain and pool our efforts, gradually increasing in numbers and in confidence. What matters is that war comes to be seen as unacceptable, that political thinking begins to shift, and that the system of militarism starts being dismantled, pushed out and replaced by new practices, treaties and structures focused on achieving genuine peace by peaceful means.[5]

REASONS FOR HOPE

Though the task ahead may seem daunting, there are grounds for encouragement. We can take heart from the goodwill and kindness of people we know and be reassured that there is a basis for human decency and compassion. We can be inspired by past movements that have succeeded in changing policies, structures and norms, however much remains to be done. We can recognise that some of the things that need to be done are in fact already happening – that we don't have to start from scratch.

The global response to the War on Terror showed that people really *do* care about things beyond their own domestic lives and immediate interests; that they *do* feel connected to people in faraway countries and are prepared to act in their defence. Among many of those who could most understandably have supported the War on Terror there has been a quite different response, illustrated by the group called 'September 11th Families for Peaceful Tomorrows'. In the heart of the country that is the current archetype of militarism, whose present leaders are committed to 'full spectrum dominance', and where national loyalty is almost a religion, there is not only a strong tradition but a growing movement of resistance.

President Bush's defence of the war on Iraq was heard in stony silence at the UN – a sign that the majority of the world's nations have had enough of the current dispensation – and the UN Secretary General has spoken plainly against unilateral military action by states and coalitions of states and for the need to give the UN its rightful authority. In the UK Tony Blair's government is paying the price for going to war without the support of the British electorate, who now see their country politically isolated.

Alongside the new resistance to militarism, the movement against the tyranny of profit grows ever stronger and is accompanied by a new level of awareness about consumer responsibility and power. That is evidence not only of a heartening degree of public knowledge and care but also of the power of ideas when they take hold.

In Latin America, a continent scarred by the excesses of militarily protected exploitation, 30 years after the assassination of President Allende in Chile, a new movement has begun to come into its own, bringing together the principles of democracy with those of social justice and responsibility. The initiatives of the radically new Brazilian government and the approach of the current leadership in Argentina give real cause for hope that there is a genuine 'third way', which has nothing to do with neo-conservatism and everything to do with respect for human beings and their needs.[6] Community and workplace resistance to the ravaging of social support by neo-liberal programmes of privatisation is growing across the continent, even in the most repressive countries.

While the globalisation of unfettered capitalism is intensifying the crisis of poverty and exclusion and threatening the very future of our planet and its ecology, another kind of globalisation is taking place. Across the world people described as ordinary are working to transform their own collective realities, locally, nationally and internationally. They are expressing their identity not through exclusive allegiances but through shared values, finding comradeship and meaning not through war but through resistance to it and working for a different kind of future. They are focused not on self-interest but on justice, finding new forms for old ideas and combining egalitarian values with those of liberty.

And wherever there is conflict – at whatever stage and level of violence – there are ordinary people working to address it: to end injustice and violence, defend human rights, build understanding and exorcise the past: from Gujarat to Bradford, from Georgia to the Philippines, from Burma to Colombia and from Bosnia to Rwanda. 'Civil society' is on the move.

The politics of identity are being challenged by the politics of identification. This is evidenced not only in the response to recent wars but, in Europe at least, in the reaction to the recent paranoia about 'asylum seekers' and immigration more generally. There is a counter-movement of people who see that as long as poverty and war are endemic, migration will be a valid human response; who recognise and uphold the dignity of their fellow human beings and indeed the need of Europeans for the lives, skills and hard work that new residents contribute.

This shift away from an entrenched culture of differentiation is coupled with the growth of new approaches to gender that challenge the old stereotypes of femininity and masculinity. Women across the world are beginning to find their voice and power. Men are finding new ways of understanding and expressing their own humanity.

It seems we have not yet woken up to the magnitude of the ecological crisis that our careless over-consumption has created. Yet at the same time the thinking of ecologists has changed our self-understanding irreversibly and awakened us to the fact of interdependence within a wider system. It seems unlikely that this will not make us more respectful of life, as a whole, and more aware of each other as fellow-beings.

Although the war on Iraq went ahead despite massive protest, the size of international mobilisation against it represented a new level of public awareness and feeling about the direction of international affairs. The fact that the argument has continued since the war (in theory) ended shows that the opposition was not superficial or ephemeral. It created a hope that people organising across the world could do something to counter the apparently overwhelming dominance of the US-based military-industrial complex or the so-called single superpower. The idea of a 'second superpower' is beginning to take hold – the global alliance of people who are ready to get out on the streets and demand change; who are no longer willing to remain passive while the power-mad wreck their world.[7]

The current political ferment has created a moment of opportunity and the real possibility that a broad peace movement will grow in strength and conviction, on the basis of a kind of activism that transcends old ideological frameworks and battles. While different factions struggle for dominance at the national level, local groups get on with the work regardless of old allegiances.

During the Iraq war several local authorities in the UK and the US were persuaded by constituents to adopt policies and pass resolutions for peace and against war. In the aftermath of the war, the city of Coventry's declaring itself a City of Peace and Reconciliation illustrates the continuation of this movement.

While it is often argued that local politics should be confined to local issues, it is a healthy sign that the connections between local and global needs and responsibilities are being made. The local borough is an ideal arena for activism on a human scale, whether on economic, environmental or peace issues. To begin acting in these ways is to start living the vision of a participatory, nonviolent society.

The very degree of public alienation from politics is creating an awareness that we have to find different ways of doing things. In the week in which I am writing this the British Home Secretary has talked in a radio interview[8] about the need for participation and the Chancellor has spoken to the Labour Party Conference of recreating community in a globalised world. They are saying these things because they know they will resonate with their listeners. Whatever one's degree of cynicism about politicians, that in itself is a good sign.

In the UK a new feature of this public resistance to militarism, which not only produced massive demonstrations but brought towns and cities to a halt (as indeed they did in some parts of the US), was the substantial participation of young people – schoolchildren in particular. This is a generation alienated by party politics but clearly concerned about the state of the world they are inheriting and willing to do something to change it.

I believe that the current vigour of the peace movement is commensurate with the misery and anger, fear and helplessness that people have felt as the world war rhetoric and war-making have increased and levels of terrorism have continued to grow. Those negative emotions have been converted into fuel for protest. In the longer run, however, if we are to protect our health and convert protest into a positive agenda, we are going to need a different kind of energy, that comes from our capacity to imagine a different outcome, a better future. It is our belief in such a possibility that can make it attainable.

What is needed is 'psychological mobilisation'[9] to bring about a fundamental shift in popular attitudes to war and peace – one that politicians will be forced to take into account. The globalisation of communications is proving invaluable for activists, making it possible to address global problems through global networks. A worldwide conversation about these issues is already in full swing on the internet. Hard-hitting newspaper articles abound. Even the BBC, until now seen as an 'Establishment' institution, has entered the debate. We must ensure that it is a debate that gets to the heart of the matter.

History is not just what happens to people but what they do and what they create. Things do change, because people come to see them as not 'normal' but wrong and act to change them. For that reason slavery was abolished, though it needs to be abolished again. Torture, once commonplace in every society, though it is still practised, is recognised as an outrage against humanity. The acceptance of war is contrary to all humane and democratic principles. It undermines the ethics that hold societies together and the value we put on human life and dignity. It destroys the lives of countless people, undoes all the good work of development, poisons the air and lays waste the land. It threatens the very future of our planet and its inhabitants. It is not normal but rather an outrage and profound reproach.

Jonathan Glover insists that 'small acts of humanity reinforce the ordinary, everyday decencies out of which the large heroic acts grow'.[10] They establish the moral ground. We need to make the connection between personal decency and kindness and the world of collective action. If we fail to do so, we leave the way open for tyranny. To take our humanity seriously means taking part in recreating human society and relegating war to the history books. Small acts of participation will help build the ground not only for heroic acts of resistance and self-giving but for a movement that is itself heroic in size and in impact.

In a BBC Radio programme celebrating the fortieth anniversary of Martin Luther King's most famous speech,[11] Alice Walker said, 'When I hear the mountain top speech I long more than ever for the time and the place to be right again.' The time *is* right, now, for dreams, for protest and for radical change. The place is everywhere. Whoever we are and wherever we live, it is up to us. We have everything to win and the price of losing is unthinkable.

Everyone Sang

Everyone suddenly burst out singing;
And I was filled with such delight
As prisoned birds must find in freedom,
Winging wildly across the white
Orchards and dark-green fields; on – on – and out
  of sight.

Everyone's voice was suddenly lifted;
And beauty came like the setting sun:
My heart was shaken with tears; and horror
Drifted away .... O, but Everyone
Was a bird; and the song was wordless; the singing will
  never be done.

Siegfried Sassoon, April 1919

Notes and References

INTRODUCTION

1. Diana Francis, *People, Peace and Power: Conflict Transformation in Action* (London: Pluto Press, 2002).
2. Friedrich Glasl, *Confronting Conflict: A First-aid Kit for Handling Conflict* (Stroud: Hawthorn Press, 1999).
3. I have used inverted commas around 'War on Terror' here to show that I consider the phrase to be spurious. I will not annoy the reader by their use hereafter but will retain the capital letters to indicate a phrase and course of action chosen by others. Please note that I shall use inverted commas variously throughout the book to distance myself from the assumptions implicit in certain words. In places that is very often.
4. Professor Sir Joseph Rotblat FRS, Nobel Peace Prize Laureate.
5. Jonathan Glover, *Humanity: a Moral History of the Twentieth Century* (London: Pimlico, 2001).
6. Glover, *Humanity*, p. 29.

CHAPTER 1

1. Source: Oxford Research Group.
2. Bath Stop the War Coalition, http://www.BathStopWar.org.uk
3. Source: Oxford Research Group.
4. Source: Report published on 9 October 2003 by Amnesty International, Oxfam and IANSA, under the title *Global Arms Trade Dangerously Unregulated*. Available on website: www.controlarms.org
5. President Dwight D. Eisenhower, *Farewell Address to the Nation* (17 January 1961).
6. Interview with US Army General Wallace on BBC Radio 4 (March 2003).
7. Interview with Gunter Grass on BBC Radio 4's *Today* programme (4 April 2003).
8. Comedian Mark Steele in the film *Not in My Name* (London: TV Choice, 2002).

CHAPTER 2

1. Michael Meacher, 'This War on Terrorism is Bogus', *Guardian* (6 September 2003).
2. *Channel 4 News* (evening of 27 October 2003).
3. George Bush in a speech to US troops in Qatar (5 June 2003).
4. BBC Radio 4's *PM* programme (20 August 2003).

5. Definition taken from *Oxford English Dictionary* 2nd edition, CD-ROM v 3.0 (Oxford University Press, 2002).
6. Hugh Miall, Oliver Ramsbotham and Tom Woodhouse, *Contemporary Conflict Resolution* (Cambridge: Polity, 1999) pp. 30–1.
7. Mats Berdal and David Malone (eds), *Greed and Grievance. Economic Agendas in Civil Wars* (Boulder, Colorado and London: Lynne Rienner, 2000).
8. Brian Ferguson, 'The Birth of War', *Natural History* (July/August 2003) pp. 28–34, p. 34.
9. Christian Aid report, *Fuelling Poverty – Oil, War and Corruption* (www. christianaid.org.uk, May 2003).
10. David Keen, 'Conflict, Trade and Economic Agendas', *CCTS Newsletter*, No. 19 (Winter 2002/03).
11. 'Living in fear' [Report from Bujumbura], *Economist* (17 July 2003).
12. Dubravka Ugresic, *The Culture of Lies* (London: Phoenix, 1998).
13. Judith Large, *The War Next Door* (Stroud: Hawthorn Press, 1997).
14. Manfred Max-Neef, 'Reflections on a Paradigm Shift in Economics', in Mary Inglis and Sandra Kramer (eds), *The New Economic Agenda* (Inverness: Findhorn Press, 1985).
15. Jonathan Glover, *Humanity: a Moral History of the Twentieth Century* (London: Pimlico, 2001).
16. Bill C. Davis, *Thomas Merton and a Chip in the Brain* (CommonDreams. org, 30 August 2002).
17. Michael Howard, *The Invention of Peace and the Reinvention of War* (London: Profile Books, 2001) p. 37.
18. BBC Radio 4's *The World at One* (23 July 2003).
19. For a discussion of this new justification for war, see the quarterly *Peace Review*, Vol. 8, No. 4 (December 1996).
20. Howard Clark, *Civil Resistance in Kosovo* (London and Sterling, Virginia: Pluto Press, 2000).
21. The British Legion advertises itself in the run-up to 'poppy day' as an organisation supporting 'those who fought, and continue to fight, for peace'.
22. Johan Galtung, discussed in Miall et al., *Contemporary Conflict Resolution*.
23. The Bible: Matthew, Chapter 7, verse 16.
24. *Guardian* (1 February 2003) p. 5.
25. *Third World Network* (11 April 2003).
26. John Latimer, *Deception in War* (London: John Murray, 2001).
27. Dr Andrew McCulloch, Chief Executive of the Mental Health Foundation, *Guardian* (Guardian Letters, 24 May 2003).
28. Naomi Goodman, former president of the Jewish Peace Fellowship.
29. Evan Davies, Economics Editor of BBC Radio 4, on Radio 4's *Thought for the Day* (25 April 2003).
30. *Guardian* (3 May 2003).

CHAPTER 3

1. Riane Eisler, *The Chalice and the Blade: Our History, Our Future* (London: Unwin Paperbacks, 1990).

2. For seminal discussions of power and its forms, see Kenneth Boulding, *Ecodynamics* (London: Sage, 1978) and Stephen Lukes, *Power: A Radical View* (London and Basingstoke: Macmillan, 1974).
3. Johan Galtung, 'Cultural Violence', *Journal of Peace Research*, Vol. 27, No. 3, 1990, pp. 291–305.
4. For an interesting discussion of ethics and economics, see Paul Strathern, *Dr. Strangelove's Game* (London: Hamish Hamilton, 2001).
5. President Dwight D. Eisenhower, *Farewell Address to the Nation*, 17 January 1961.
6. Michael Moore, *Stupid White Men* (London: Penguin Books, 2002).
7. Christian Aid report, *Fuelling Poverty – Oil, War and Corruption* (www.christianaid.org.uk, May 2003).
8. Arundhati Roy, *Confronting Empire*, Porto Alegre, Brazil, 27 January 2003.
9. George Ryan, former Republican Governor of Illinois, in an interview on BBC Radio 4's *Today* programme (6 May 2003).
10. Sven Lindqvist, *Exterminate All the Brutes* (London: Granta Books, 1997).
11. Titus Alexander, *Unravelling Global Apartheid* (Cambridge: Polity Press, 1996).
12. Conn Hallinan, *US and India – Dangerous Alliance*, Portside's internet service (10 May 2003).
13. Richard Dawkins, *The Selfish Gene* (Oxford: Oxford Paperbacks, 1989).
14. Frans de Waal, *Good Natured: the Origins of Right and Wrong in Humans and Other Animals* (Cambridge, MA: Harvard University Press, 1997).
15. John Keegan, *A History of Warfare* (London: Pimlico, 1994); Eisler, *The Chalice and the Blade*; Elise Boulding, *Cultures of Peace: The Hidden Side of History* (New York: Syracuse University Press, 2000).
16. Galtung, 'Cultural Violence'.
17. Galtung, 'Cultural Violence', p. 291.
18. A US nuclear submarine was named *Corpus Christi*.
19. Becky Francis, *Power Plays: Primary School Children's Constructions of Gender, Power and Adult Work* (Stoke on Trent: Trentham Books, 1998).
20. Jonathan Glover, *Humanity: a Moral History of the Twentieth Century* (London: Pimlico, 2001) p. 52.
21. BBC Radio 4's *Today* programme (11 December 2003).
22. Riane Eisler, *Sacred Pleasure* (San Francisco: Harper San Francisco, 1995).
23. Eisler, *The Chalice and The Blade*.
24. Raymond Kelly, *Warless Societies and the Origin of War* (Michigan: University of Michigan Press, 2000).
25. Dylan Mathews, *War Prevention Works* (Oxford: The Oxford Research Group, 2001).
26. Eisler, *Sacred Pleasure*, p. 375.
27. Glover, *Humanity*, p. 414.
28. Carol Gilligan, *In a Different Voice* (Cambridge, MA: Harvard University Press, 1982).
29. Michael Billig, *Arguing and Thinking* (Cambridge: Cambridge University Press, 1987).
30. Eisler, *Sacred Pleasure*.

31. Aleksandr Solzhenitsyn, *The Gulag Archipelago (1918–1956)*, translated by Thomas P. Whitney and Harry Willets (New York: The Harvill Press, 1988).
32. Eisler, *Sacred Pleasure*; Owen Flanagan, 'The colour of happiness', *New Scientist* (24 May 2003) p. 44; Ken Wilber, *A Theory of Everything* (Dublin: Gateway, 2001).
33. Oliver McTernan, *Violence in God's Name: the Role of Religion in an Age of Conflict* (London: Darton, Longman and Todd, 2003).
34. The Quaker founder George Fox was quoted by a contemporary, Margaret Fell, as saying: 'You will say Christ saith this, and the apostles say this; but what canst thou say?'
35. Eisler, *Sacred Pleasure*.
36. Michael Nicholson, *ITV News* (7 April 2003) on the assault on Baghdad.
37. George Robertson, former NATO General Secretary, in an interview on BBC Radio 4's *Today* programme (14 May 2003).

CHAPTER 4

1. Immanuel Kant, *The Metaphysics of Morals*, trans. Mary Gregor (Cambridge: Cambridge University Press, 1991).
2. Friedrich Nietzsche, *Basic Writings*, trans. Walter Kaufman (New York: Random House, 1967).
3. For an excellent discussion of different sources and forms of power, see Kenneth Boulding, *Ecodynamics* (London: Sage, 1978).
4. Jonathan Glover, *Humanity: a Moral History of the Twentieth Century* (London: Pimlico, 2001) pp. 69, 70.
5. Arundhati Roy, *Operation Iraqi Freedom? I Don't Think So* (Third World Network, 11 April 2003).
6. St Augustine, *The City of God*, trans. M. Dods (New York: Random House, 1950).
7. Michael Walzer, *Just and UnJust Wars* (London: Pelican, 1980).
8. Walzer, *Just and Unjust Wars*.
9. Mike Garnier, *Peace News* (Letters, 12 November 1980).
10. Source: Scilla Elworthy, Oxford Research Group (personal communication).
11. Simon Blackburn, *Being Good: a Short Introduction to Ethics* (Oxford: OUP, 2001).
12. Walzer, *Just and Unjust Wars*.
13. Blackburn, *Being Good*.
14. Kant, *The Metaphysics of Morals*.
15. John Hooper, 'Germans wrestle with rights and wrongs of torture', *Guardian*, 27 February 2003, p. 18.
16. Isaiah Berlin, 'My Intellectual Path', *New York Review*, 14 May 1998, pp. 53–60.
17. Michael Randle (ed.), *Challenge to Nonviolence*, University of Bradford, Department of Peace Studies, Issues of Peace Research 2002.
18. Brazilian President Luiz Inacio Lula da Silva's Speech at the G-8 Summit in Evian, translated by Narco News (2 June 2003).

19. Antoine de Saint-Exupéry, *Wind, Sand and Stars* (London: Penguin, 1995): a book that is one long reflection on humanity and the human condition.
20. John Burton (ed.), *Conflict: Human Needs Theory* (London: Macmillan, 1990).
21. Roger Lewin, *Complexity: Life at the Edge of Chaos* (London: Phoenix, 2001).
22. Some further reading on the concept of Just War: Jenny Teichman, *Pacifism and the Just War: a Study in Applied Philosophy* (Oxford and New York: Blackwell,1986); A. E. Harvey, *Demanding Peace: Christian Responses to War and Violence* (London: SCM Press, 1999); D. Rodin, *War and Self-Defense* (Oxford: Clarendon Press, 2003): R. Norman, *Ethics, Killing and War* (Cambridge: Cambridge University Press, 1955).

CHAPTER 5

1. I am indebted for this idea to Oliver Ramsbotham and Tom Woodhouse. Though it came to me through personal communication it will be included in the forthcoming second edition of Miall, Ramsbotham and Woodhouse, *Contemporary Conflict Resolution* (Cambridge: Polity Press, 1999).
2. Samuel P. Oliner and Pearl M. Oliner, *The Altruistic Personality: Rescuers of Jews in Nazi Europe* (New York: Macmillan, 1992).
3. For instance, Stephen King-Hall, *Defence in the Nuclear Age* (London: Gollancz, 1959); Brian Martin, *Uprooting War* (London: Freedom Press, 1984); Theodor Ebert, *'Soziale Verteidigung', Vol.1: Historische Erfahrungen und Grundsätze der Strategie* (Waldkirch: Waldkircher Verlag, 1996); Gene Sharp, *There Are Realistic Alternatives* (Boston: The Albert Einstein Institution, 2003); Roger S. Powers, William B. Vogele, Christopher Kruegler, and Ronald M. McCarthy, *Protest, Power, and Change: an Encyclopedia of Nonviolent Action from ACT-UP to Women's Suffrage* (New York: Garland, 1997).
4. James Scott, *Domination and the Hidden Arts of Resistance* (Yale: Yale University Press, 1990).
5. Mohandas was Gandhi's first name. Mahatma is a courtesy title.
6. Michael Randle, *Eastern & East Central Europe: Part I The Establishment and Erosion of Communist Power* and *Part II: People Power Revolutions in East Central Europe, 1989* (Notes for students from Colgate University, New York State to the Department of Peace Studies, Bradford University, 2002).
7. For an excellent brief account see Patrick Burke, *Revolution in Europe in 1989* (Hove, East Sussex: Wayland, 1995).
8. Hannah Arendt was an important thinker on the desirability and pitfalls of people's action. For a helpful summary, see Margaret Canovan, *Hannah Arendt: a Reinterpretation of Her Political Thought* (Cambridge: Cambridge University Press, 1992).
9. Adolfo Perez Esquivel, *Christ in a Poncho* (Maryknoll NY: Orbis Books, 1983).

10. *A Force More Powerful: a Century of Nonviolent Conflict*, a brilliant series of TV programmes, available as videos, documenting nonviolent struggles in different parts of the world (Washington DC: York Zimmerman and WETA).

11. For an inspiring human account read Howell Raines, *My Soul is Rested: Movement Days in the Deep South Remembered* (New York: Penguin Books, 1983).

12. For more on people's action for peace, see Dylan Mathews, *War Prevention Works: 50 Stories of People Resolving Conflict* (Oxford: Oxford Research Group, 2001) and the ACCORD series published by Conciliation Resources.

13. BBC Radio 4's *Today* programme (23 July 2003).

14. Jo Wilding, *Solidarity and Destruction* (www.wildfirejo.org.uk, 24 November 2003).

15. See www.peacebrigades.org

16. Dr Hanan Ashrawi's Sydney Peace Prize address on Peace in the Middle East: 'A Global Challenge and a Human Imperative'.

17. For more information on the OSCE see their website www.osce.org and Paul Van Tongeren, Hans Van de Veen and Juliette Verhoeven, *Searching for Peace in Europe and Eurasia* (Boulder, CO: Lynne Rienner, 2002) pp. 546–51.

18. Scilla Elworthy, Oxford Research Group, *Alternatives to War*. Notes for a presentation at a meeting of Bristol Stop the War Coalition and others (Folk House, Bristol, 21 September 2003).

19. Michael Howard, *The Invention of Peace and the Reinvention of War* (London: Profile Books, 2001) p. 37.

CHAPTER 6

1. Henry Louis Gates Jnr., 'A Liberalism that Dares to Speak its Name', *International Herald Tribune* (30 March 1994): 'the challenge is to move from a politics of identity to a politics of identification'.

2. See Michael Moore's film, *Bowling for Columbine*, about the level of gun crime in the US and the role of fear.

3. Brian Ferguson, 'The Birth of War', *Natural History* (July/August 2003) pp. 28–34.

4. Howard Zinn, *My Country: The World*, published on Monday 3 May 2003 by TomPaine.com

5. Clifford Geertz, *The Interpretation of Cultures* (London: Hutchinson, 1975).

6. Or in a desert. See Antoine de Saint-Exupery, *Wind, Sand and Stars* (first published in French in 1939 as *Terre des Hommes*) (London: Penguin, 1995) p. 102.

7. Colin Tudge, 'Why nasty guys rule and nice guys let them', *New Statesman*, 11 August 2003, pp. 17–19.

8. The thinking of 'deep ecology' is relevant here. See, for instance, A. Naess (D. Rothberg trans.), *Ecology, Community and Lifestyle: Outline of an Ecosophy* (Cambridge: Cambridge University Press, 1990).

9. Eva Hoffman, *Lost in Translation* (London: William Heinemann, 1989) p. 276.
10. I am indebted to Peter Reason for the notion of participation. See his Inaugural Professorial Lecture, 'Justice, Sustainability, and Participation' (published in *Concepts and Transformations*, Vol. 7, No. 1, 2002) pp. 7–29.
11. Definition taken from the *Oxford English Dictionary*, 2nd edition, CD-ROM v3.0 (Oxford University Press, 2002).
12. 'Conscientised' is the word used by the radical educationalist, Paulo Freire, in *Pedagogy of the Oppressed* (London: Penguin, 1972).
13. Michael Billig, *Banal Nationalism* (London: Sage, 1995).
14. George Lakey, *Afflicting the Comfortable: Alex Wood Memorial Lecture*, Fellowship of Reconciliation (8 February 1970).
15. Barbara Deming, 'On Revolution and Equilibrium', New York, A. J. Muste Institute. Reprinted from *Liberation Magazine* (February 1968).
16. This was written before Tony Blair's 'big conversation' came on the scene!

CHAPTER 7

1. The statement of purpose of War Resisters International (www.wri-irg. org).
2. Philip Morrison, *Powers of ten* (New York: Scientific American Library, 1982).
3. For an international directory of organisations working against war and for peace, see *Housman's Annual Peace Diary*, available from Housman's Bookshop in London.
4. Jonathan Glover, *Humanity: a Moral History of the Twentieth Century* (London: Pimlico, 2001).
5. Johan Galtung, *Peace by Peaceful Means* (London, Thousand Oaks CA and New Delhi: Sage, 1996).
6. William Greider and Kenneth Rapoza, 'Lula Raises the Stakes', *The Nation* (1 December 2003).
7. On 17 February 2003, in a front page article of the *New York Times*, Patrick Tyler described the global anti-war protests as the emergence of 'the second superpower'. And on 31 March 2003 James F. Moore (Berkman Center for Internet & Society) wrote a piece entitled 'The Second Superpower Rears its Beautiful Head'. See: http://cyber.law.harvard.edu/people/jmoore/secondsuperpower.html
8. Interview with David Blunkett on BBC Radio 4's *Today* programme (24 September 2003).
9. Guram Odisharia, *The Pass of the Persecuted* (Tbilisi: Foundation Alex, 2001).
10. Glover, *Humanity*, p. 393.
11. BBC Radio 4's *Book of the Week* programme, Martin Luther King: a tribute (28 August 2003).

Index

Compiled by Peter Ellis